THE RAINBOW THROUGH THE RAIN

THE RAINBOW
THROUGH THE RAIN

GEOFFREY SCOTT MOWAT

NEW CHERWELL PRESS · OXFORD

First published in Great Britain 1995
by New Cherwell Press
7 Mount Street, Oxford OX2 6DH
Copyright © 1995 G.S. Mowat

British Library Cataloguing-in-Publication Data
A catalogue record for this book
is available from the British Library

ISBN 0-951-7695-9-6

Cover design by Philip Carr
Printed in Malta by Interprint

Dedication

To my children and flock of grandchildren

Acknowledgement and thanks

To Louise, for encouraging me to write up the account of my attempted escape, during balmy days crossing the Indian Ocean, December 1945, and for her part in the writing of the book fifty years later.

I express grateful thanks to friends and former colleagues in the Malayan Civil Service who contributed various items in the Index and Glossary, and in partciular to Jim Rae (J.T. Rae, CMG, M.C.S. retired) who helped in the compilation and checking of the same.

O LOVE THAT WILL NOT LET ME GO

Words by G. Matheson, 1842-1906

O Love that will not let me go,
　　I rest my weary soul in thee:
I give thee back the life I owe,
That in thine ocean depths its flow
　　May richer, fuller, be.

O Light that followest all my way,
　　I yield my flickering torch to thee:
My heart restores its borrowed ray,
That in thy sunshine's blaze its day
　　May brighter, fairer, be.

O Joy that seekest me through pain,
　　I cannot close my heart to thee:
I trace the rainbow through the rain
And feel the promise is not vain
　　That morn shall tearless be.

O Cross that liftest up my head,
　　I dare not ask to fly from thee:
I lay in dust life's glory dead,
And from the ground there blossoms red
　　Life that shall endless be.

CONTENTS

PREFACE

One evening when I was at boarding school the Matron gathered some of us older girls and we had tea together. Afterwards she said: 'Shall I tell the teacups for you?' and we agreed. So we turned our teacups upside down in the saucers to see what the leaves would say. When it came to my turn the Matron looked at the pattern at the bottom of the cup and said: 'Oh, you're going to marry a parson!' My face fell and I was horrified, for the last thing I wanted was to marry a parson.

When I went to College, therefore, and met Geof I was pleased, and felt quite secure as he intended to go abroad, in the Indian Civil Service perhaps, and would become a District Officer, and I felt that I would like to follow him in doing that.

I am writing this because Geof's call to the ministry was one of the greatest stumbling blocks in our married life, and yet God was able' to take it away in time, as you will discover in this joint adventure of a lifetime.

Louise Mowat
Wengen, Switzerland,
April 1995

INTRODUCTION

Beach post, Singapore: 10th Jan 1942.

Plumes of oily smoke, billowing up into huge clouds, were rising from what the Japanese war-planes had left of the docks and go-downs at Keppel Harbour. I could see this quite clearly from where I stood outside my pill-box to the rear of the Singapore Swimming Club. Our machine gun platoon had been deployed in beach defence since early December, strung along the narrow spit of land called Tanjong Rhu, which lay on the seaward side of Kallang aerodrome, and I was second-in-command.

The outlook was not good. Overall the strategy of the Japanese High Command had been brilliant, planning simultaneous assaults on two major Allied defence zones across the wide reaches of the South West Pacific. With consummate timing and astounding execution they had launched entirely separate attacks on the 7th/8th December 1941, one by carrier-based aircraft against the bastion of American might at the U.S. Naval Base at Pearl Harbour, Hawaii: the other, a sea-borne invasion upon the shores of Southern Thailand and Northern Malaya.

From the moment the Japanese forces landed on the beaches of Kelantan which face the China Sea, and poured across from Thailand into the fertile but ill-protected plains of Kedah on the 8th December, the pressure on British, Australian and Indian troops had been relentless. Once a foothold had been secured and the defensive line broken, the Japanese divisions moved southwards with frightening speed, continually turning the flank, leap-frogging at a great rate down the peninsula, often mounted on bicycles, using minor roads or tracks through rubber estates and causing immense confusion. Communications became increasingly difficult and many people were demoralised.

One after another the important centres fell. Penang was abandoned early on. Ipoh fell on Christmas Eve. The Japanese landed at Port Dickson two weeks later to find our beloved Malacca

1

waiting like a ripe plum for the picking. A courageous and stubborn retreat by our defending forces, especially the Australians in South Johore, had certainly delayed the enemy, but the retreat went on.

To all this must be added the demoralising effect of other factors. Firstly, the British fighter planes called Brewster Buffaloes were by then becoming obsolete and no match for the Japanese Navy Zero fighters. By mid-January there were no planes remaining on the island for the defence of the ground forces. Secondly, a devastating blow had been suffered by the sinking of two battleships, *Prince of Wales* and *Repulse*, off the East coast of the Malay Peninsula on the 10th December. Thirdly, only a week or two later, the fall of Hong Kong had effectively shown the determination as well as the might of the Japanese onslaught. For how long, then, could Singapore hold out in these circumstances?

During the past three weeks Louise had been working as a stenographer at General Headquarters, out at Sime Road. Right at the centre of things she had followed the crumbling of the British defences with alarm and was not altogether unprepared when the decision came for the withdrawal of the headquarters unit from Singapore to Java. A night or two before, when I had been given compassionate leave, she had told me about this and wondered if she should accept the chance to be evacuated from the Island with the other women if the offer were made.

Louise wanted to remain and stay with me if possible. It did not take me more than a moment however to see that this was a golden opportunity for her to escape the awful consequences of a siege and possible internment, and I told her that I thought it wise for her to go while the going was good. If she stayed she could not help me, and I could not help her — indeed she would only be an anxiety.

Reluctantly she accepted this decision and with one or two close friends at the headquarters she was ready, packed up and able to move at a moment's notice. Embarkation was to take place at 5 pm that afternoon and we parted under a cloud of anxiety and un-certainty.

I was busy thinking about this depressing situation when to my astonishment I saw Louise walking purposefully towards my post.

2

I rushed up to her impulsively and said: 'Hello! what on earth are you doing here?' 'Oh Geof,' she replied, 'I couldn't do it. I've jumped ship!'

I was momentarily dumbfounded when I saw a mischievous smile. 'Darling, I was only pulling your leg! I'm here because the sailing has been delayed twelve hours, and the Graemes dropped me off here.'

A wave of relief came over me, but Louise could not stop for more than a moment. I drew my gold signet ring off my left hand and gave it to her. 'Wear this,' I said, 'until we meet again.' We kissed and parted. I think we were both elated, but it was to be a long separation.

CHAPTER 1

CITY OF DREAMING SPIRES:
1936

How did it all begin? After all these years our time at Oxford University seems like a dream. For me it was a heady experience when my college tutorials and lectures took second place to my courtship of Louise: when the meetings between us at the Monday evening rehearsals of the Bach Choir or the rehearsals of the Oxford University Opera Club were much more important than the daily stint of reading for my degree in Modern History. Certain things had to be done. Books had to be read. Essays had to be written. There was a goal — or rather a series of goals — to be attained as a means of setting myself up in a responsible career and I had my focus on these. I had also the brimming excitement of a first love, and a girl who not only wanted to get married as soon as possible, but was eager to go abroad.

The Oxford term is only eight weeks long. Perhaps we did not know how privileged we were, but as a basis to this undergraduate life we had, in the first place, a room in college, a 'scout' or college servant to look after us, dinner in Hall five nights a week and a host of activities physical and cultural to absorb the energies of some of the liveliest people on earth, in addition to the programme of reading and lectures handed out by one's tutor.

I had rowed at school and I continued to do so at Corpus Christi until I was forced to retire with a damaged back. I joined the O.U. Officers Training Corps (Cavalry Squadron), I attended the Summer Camps and all that was tremendous fun. Through belonging to the O.U. Music Club I was able, as a 'cellist, to take the first tentative steps in chamber music and hear many fine recitals at the Holywell Music Room.

With all this there had to be a daily meeting with Louise if possible, and on Sunday mornings we would often attend the 8 o'clock communion at St. Peter's in the East (where I had been baptised) before joining friends for an organised ramble somewhere in the nearby Chiltern Hills between Oxford and London.

Louise was in her third year at St. Hugh's College when I met her, and was to take her final Schools in Greats in the Summer of 1938. In her last term we decided to get engaged. Her parents, however, were somewhat diffident about my approaches and, when I asked her father if we might be engaged, was told that this was hardly suitable as I had no job in prospect.

I admit to having been rather crestfallen at this rebuff, but we were not unduly dismayed. A few days later Louise had to go to Bath for a visit to her dentist, and I accompanied her for the outing. It was enjoyable in a way but memorable for us both, for on leaving the dentist we dropped into a jeweller's in Cheap Street and came out with an engagement ring — a moonstone set in gold which pleased us both. But Louise had to wear it on a chain round her neck!

By that time the international situation had worsened and our lives became increasingly overshadowed by the approaching war. Louise very sensibly took a six months' crash course in typing and stenography in London while I soldiered on at Oxford. This of course was very good for me, even while I found it lonely, for it enabled me to concentrate on my final year and in addition to take on the job of President of the O.U. Opera Club, which had been the cause of my engagement with Louise.

O.T.C. parades and exercises continued unabated. In due course I took my O.T.C. Certificate 'B', losing my voice through stentorian abuse of the same in pouring rain, on horseback of course, shouting orders at my troop. I failed. Rather more important, perhaps, was a singular success notched up by the Opera Club, when we performed *Dido and Aeneas* in 1938 and *The Beggars Opera* in the following year, both of them at the Oxford Playhouse, to overflowing houses.

At this point it should be explained that I attempted the Joint Home Civil Service / Indian Civil Service examination at a terrible hotel near St. Pancras Station in London in June of 1939. I was unplaced for any vacancy then, but was more fortunate when

6

interviewed for selection to the Colonial Administrative Service about the same time. I had asked for either Ceylon, Hong Kong or British Malaya, and to my amazement and jubilation was offered a Far Eastern Cadetship in the Straits Settlements. True I did not care for the rather dull postage stamps of Singapore, Penang and Malacca (the old Straits Settlements) but I had a special fondness for those issued by the Malay States, which showed the head of a fierce-looking tiger appearing through a clump of lallang grass. I thought I might find my way there in due course, and I did too, some fifteen years later!

At once the situation became brighter, positively luminous in fact. For one thing Louise and I were able to become officially engaged: secondly, on appointment to H.M. Overseas Service, together with my contemporaries I was reserved from joining up in Britain, and thirdly we were required, the following October, to take up a three-term course based at Rhodes House, Oxford, in preparation for our Colonial Service appointments. Within weeks war was declared, although to begin with, apart from the black-out, very little changed.

By this time Louise and I thought we had had quite a long enough engagement and were desperate to get married: but appointment to Malaya meant a long separation, depending on how soon I could pass the exams in language, Law etc, but very likely extending to four years when I would become eligible for my first Home Leave.

The intervening weeks between the outbreak of war with Germany and the beginning of the Oxford term were a curious form of limbo. I couldn't join up: Louise was in London engaged on her first job as a Research Assistant in what was later to become the Ministry of Information in wartime Britain. For my part, what could be more enjoyable than to spend a few weeks in Newquay, Cornwall, swimming and tennis galore, with my greatest friend from schooldays at Clifton, Tim Harris, a delightful, witty and enterprising rogue, who had brought considerable zest and adventure to the subfusc of Wadham college in his day and who had been appointed at the same time as me to the Colonial Service in Tanganyika. He was a marvellous person, and I mention him now with great affection. Tim in due course made an outstanding contribution to the administration

7

in that African Territory in senior and responsible appointments: he was also designated my best man.

I simply must introduce another great character in this story, a truly delightful person who became a friend and mentor to Louise and me at this time and who changed our lives for good. He was A.S. Haynes, CMG, who had retired from the Malayan Civil Service in 1936 as acting British Adviser at Kelantan, after a full and varied life in the Federated Malay States and Singapore. Now living in retirement in Leamington Spa, he used to travel to Oxford once a week to spend time at the Colonial Services Club in Broad Street, see the six or seven Far Eastern Cadets and take us for a class in the Malay language. Over lunch he would regale us with intriguing stories of his time in Malaya, and he appeared to me as a person of great sympathy and also an example of what I imagined a Colonial Officer should be. We soon became firm friends, and he invited Louise and me to his home in Leamington one weekend in term time.

I have already referred to the rules then in force regarding marriage, and quite naturally we expressed our longing to get married and our fears for a lengthy separation. 'Why, my dear fellow, the war has changed all that! If I were you I should write to the Governor.' And so I did! With immense presumption and a good deal of cheek I laid out my case, described what an adornment Louise would be to life in a Colonial situation etc etc, and posted the letter to H.E. the Governor of Singapore (by airmail of course. The flying boat service took about ten days).

We waited and waited. The months were slipping by. In a matter of weeks our course would come to an end. Soon I would get sailing orders and that would be that. Once again A.S. Haynes came to the rescue. 'My dear chap,' he exclaimed, 'you can't let this go on. Send a cable!' To our astonishment and relief, within ten days or so I received a cable in reply.

Mr Mowat is given permission to marry. He should however be aware that his salary as an unpassed Cadet may prove to be insufficient to maintain a married establishment. His wife would be required to pay her own passage.

What more could we possibly desire? My parents were delighted, Louise's warmly supported the arrangement, supposing their daughter would be much safer in the Far East, and most generously gave a present which more than met the cost of her passage.

No sooner had we laid plans for a simple wedding, at St. Peter's in the East, Oxford, when I received orders — standby for departure, port of embarkation as yet unspecified, on the 15th July 1940, and rushed to get our special licence. The wedding was on the 6th July and we could not have been more grateful to Mr Haynes for thus transforming the situation, to begin our life in Malaya as a married if still very green young couple!

CHAPTER 2

HALCYON DAYS

Malacca 1940-41

There is nothing more exciting than a longed-for landfall. We had been at sea for nearly seven weeks, sailing round the Cape of Good Hope and across the Indian Ocean. We had stopped briefly at Capetown and Mombasa, but these visits had merely served to whet our appetites for the tropical experience proper. A couple of days in Colombo was a foretaste, but to find ourselves at anchor at Georgetown, Penang, on 20th September and to espy the noble outline of Kedah Peak through our porthole seemed very heaven!

There was hardly time to do more there than to have our first ride in a ricksha, pulled by a Chinese whose knotted and varicosed legs still haunt me, and to sample our first manggisteens, those wonderful little fruits whose tiny liths within their purple shells afford the finest flavour of any tropical fruit I know.

Within a few hours we were steaming South to Singapore, with a magical arrival shortly after dawn, when we all crowded on deck to wonder at the beauty of the harbour entrance between a multitude of sparkling islets.

That very day my fate was to be sealed, together with that of my fellow-cadets, and we were all anxious as to where we might be sent. The possibilities lay between the Malay, the Chinese and the Tamil sides. Malay cadets might have appeared to have a better general chance on the administrative side, particularly in district appointments. Those chosen to learn a Chinese dialect would have to spend two years in China, either Macao or Amoy (for Cantonese or Hokkien respectively), and then possibly face a somewhat restricted career within what was at that time called the Chinese Protectorate. The least attractive possibility was to be detailed to learn Tamil (or rarely Telegu) which meant a year's stay in South

India and thereafter posting for duties mainly in the Labour Department. Mowat, believed to be musical, who could distinguish and even imitate tones uttered as examples of a Chinese dialect, might well have been picked out for language study in China. But he was married, so that was ruled out. There was only one posting where married quarters were then available – the District Office, Alor Gajah, Malacca. I was to be a Malay Cadet after all, much envied by the others, and I returned elated to the Adelphi Hotel to bring the good news to Louise. What was more, our sympathetic Establishment Officer, John Peel, very kindly arranged that we should proceed to Malacca by the next Straits Steamship, instead of taking the Night Mail via Tampin.

What could be more romantic than an overnight voyage up the coast to our first assignment, sitting on deck under the brilliant starlit sky? And so it turned out. The Harbour Master, Frank Smith, later a great friend, turned out in his launch at dawn to bring us ashore and convey us to the Residency. His welcome was warm and friendly enough. We wondered, however, what the Resident Councillor would say when we met over breakfast. We drank tea and ate fruit brought to us on the verandah upstairs, and then came down. The Resident Councillor was kindly. His wife was more astringent. To Louise she said: 'I suppose you have private means?' It was clear she was afraid we might let the side down.

In retrospect those early months at Alor Gajah, when I was learning the language and the work and Louise was learning to be a Colonial 'mem', are like a golden age before our innocence was shattered by the trauma of the Japanese war and our lengthy separation. Our Malayan honeymoon extended a little over twelve months, but remains quite unforgettable.

At the District Office, first under a bit of a martinet, A.D. York, and then under a milder type, Guy Turner, I was broken in gently to the style of a land office of the Straits Settlements, in perhaps the best era of Colonial administration. Everything to do with the collection of Land Revenue, registration of titles for land, applications for new land (not much available in this well-settled part of the Peninsula) was meticulously seen to, and in this I was guided by a young Malay clerk, Haji Noordin bin Haji Matsom, who had made himself an expert in the complex local land procedures which were subject to the 'adat perpateh' – that is the customary law regarding inheritance in this strongly matriarchal area. In addition, as soon as I had passed my first law exam I was gazetted Magistrate Class II, and sat on the Bench to deal with minor offences and preliminary enquiries, two or three days a week.

Two incidents stick in my mind in regard to the Court work. The first had to do with the prosecution by the Protector of Chinese of a certain Chinese towkay who was alleged to have kept a little girl as a 'mui tsai' or slave-of-all-work, something forbidden in the enlightened days of Colonial rule. While everything seemed to point to the guilt of the towkay in the harsh conditions of this small girl's world, there was one matter which might afford him an escape. The question was: did he, when it came to Chinese New Year, allow his slavey to return to her family, or not? The reply came: he did. I dismissed the case.

The other incident arose out of a somewhat embarrassing relationship with a Malaccan lawyer called Salt. I might groan inwardly when I saw him in Court – he was often retained to defend quite simple cases – but when it came to one o'clock and the adjournment of Court until 2.15, my conscience would not let me see him sit in his car, or take a bite at the local coffee shop. I had to invite him to lunch as there was no government Rest House in the village.

In the course of time Mr Salt wished to repay our hospitality, so on a convenient public holiday we accepted an invitation to spend a day at his seaside chalet along the coast at Tanjong Bidara. The tide was in, the waters of the Straits no muddier than usual, so we went in for a bathe before lunch. As I waded into the shallow water I was aware of a few tiny prickles, but a moment later rocked back in excruciating pain as the tentacles of some nasty creature wrapped themselves round my leg. I tore up the beach to the little shack, the others rushing up at my cries. I was in agony and nothing would allay the terrific pain – not even neat whisky which the frightened Salt tried to rub over the affected leg. Better drink it, Louise said.

The sting of a Portuguese Man-of-War was reputed dangerous, sometimes fatal if the long, streaming tentacles happened to encircle one's body. In my case, since the pain seemed to increase rather than diminish, the best thing seemed, whatever the danger, for Louise to drive me with all speed to hospital. We set off to cover the ten or twelve miles in record time, while with every breath I felt my end draw nearer. The poison from the stings was affecting my breathing. 'Do you know,' I gasped, 'how to give artificial respiration?' In the event it wasn't necessary. I had a couple of stiff injections at the General Hospital and was kept in for 24 hours. For weeks afterwards I could not bear to wear a sock or shoe on that leg and for several months I was distinctly allergic to any form of seafood!

Louise and I had sailed away from England a few weeks after the miracle of Dunkirk. The Battle of Britain was approaching its climax. Churchill was declaiming his finest speeches. In August of 1940 the Government of the Straits Settlements had finally brought in conscription of certain categories of persons. I was among them, and so it was that within a few days of arrival in the country I was duly called up, enrolled willy-nilly in the Malacca Battalion of the S.S. Volunteer Force and hauled off for a special camp for newly 'embodied' expatriates like myself at the training camp at Tanjong Kling, some miles out of Malacca.

The weeks and months flew past. Part of the joy was an ever-expanding range of experience whether walking the narrow bunds dividing the rice paddies with a headman, exploring the niceties of the Malay language with my munshi, or sweating up a jungle path to a minor summit in the foothills of the Central Range.

Every few weeks there would be a Volunteer camp. The need for better training was of course important, and yet what should have been our proper role – behind the lines operations – was completely ignored. It became rather tedious to break down our machine guns and reassemble them in a race against the next section. For example dealing with a stoppage, while firing, started with the drill order 'clear the round off the face of the extractor'. We roared with laughter when my friend and colleague in the M.C.S., Tony Mills, called out: 'Wipe the smile off the face of the instructor.'

13

In late November 1941 that smile quite disappeared as the threat from the Japanese forces building up in Thailand became more and more evident. We could no longer go on pretending that we would somehow not be caught up in the ever-increasing scope of war, but until it came upon us the wheels of administration would go on turning, and if our turn for local leave was due, we decided we would take it and make the most of what might be our last visit to Frasers Hill for a long, long time.

CHAPTER 3

MOBILISATION!

That Friday was a day of darkness and rain. Not ordinary darkness and not ordinary rain, for both are etched upon my memory as marking a special moment in time. What came before had been one thing. There was light and joy and the excitement of loving and being loved in the uncertain world of the 1940s, as well as so much of fear and uncertainty as the events of those stark and graceless years embroiled the nations in the second World War.

The darkness which Louise and I were feeling was more than the darkness of a tropical night. The rain which pelted against the windscreen of our small car as we hugged the hairpin bends coming down from Frasers Hill was the presage of the monsoon – the North East Monsoon which breaks regularly upon the Malay Peninsula towards the end of November. The darkness and the rain cut off what had gone before. It was as if a curtain had come down upon our life. What came after would be a different thing – if there was to be any after. And at that moment it did not bear thinking about.

It was Friday the 26th November, and how should I ever forget it? Louise and I had taken a few days' leave. We had driven from Alor Gajah to Kuala Lumpur, crossed the Central Range at the Ginting Simpah by the winding road leading down to Pahang and to Kuala Lipis, some 200 miles in all, to stay awhile with Jack and Patricia Hayward. The news which came through the Residency at Lipis was disturbing, but we stuck to our plans and two days later took the hill road by way of Raub up to the Gap where we had booked in at the Rest House.

We were fond of the place and had been twice already to this little bit of England perched some 2000 feet above the steamy plains of Selangor, where dahlias and roses were encouraged to grow and where the Indian gardener would bring in freshly-picked runner beans to go with the roast chicken. It was cold enough in the evenings for a fire, for there was always a keen wind blowing across the pass between Selangor and Pahang, and we could enjoy it. But that evening there was little comfort and small enjoyment. Indeed all we had was a hasty meal and the unwelcome summons to return to Malacca at once, late as it was, since a telephone message from the Adjutant of my battalion instructed me to proceed immediately to Volunteer Headquarters. A week later our battalion was on its way to Singapore Island.

Amazingly, six letters which I wrote 'On Active Service' in Singapore to Louise, while she remained at Alor Gajah, have survived to this day, some written from Sub-sector Headquarters, some 'on patrol' and one from the Guard Room. This last is of peculiar interest as it relates the unhappy circumstances of my being charged with the loss of 45 rounds of ·303 ammunition. It was taken while I was asleep on a rare night in camp, and I can remember being so overcome that I found nothing to say in my defence. The C.O., Col. T.H. Newey, sentenced me to seven days Field Punishment as described in the following extract:

Camp 19/12/41

Life has been a bit trying during the past few days, and will continue to be so for a while I fear. On Tuesday I had the misfortune to lose some 45 rounds of ammunition, I don't know how. My whole bandolier went, and I think someone must have pinched it. Anyhow after a lot of susah I was put under open arrest, and was remanded by O'Grady to the C.O. who condemned me to seven days field punishment (hard labour). I wept over it, but now I have settled down to it I'm trying to bear up philosophically.

Yesterday the first real day was agony. Shifting boxes, pickets, loading trucks, shifting more pickets. I nearly passed out in the hot sun. The R.S.M. stands over us and now I know what it is like to be in a Chain Gang. There is one other with me, a Malay, oddly enough one of the teachers at Alor Gajah! He bore the heat better than me but confessed he nearly 'pitam' (passed out). A drink of water saved me in the nick of time.

16

My seven days 'hard' I may say won me considerable sympathy among my fellows, the more so when it came to light that the C.O. had exceeded his powers in awarding the sentence without the formalities of a court-martial. Looking at it now, considering that the enemy was half-way down the Peninsula, it seems quite absurd, but on the good side it toughened me up and was over by the time Louise decided it was pointless to stay any longer at Alor Gajah, and drove down with a few cherished possessions to Singapore.

This decision, in fact, was reached partly through a telegram which I asked my cousin Tony Loch to send while I was serving sentence, and I have enclosed a copy of it as it is a truly fascinating piece of family history as well as a miracle of survival.

By now it was Christmas Day. I was a free man. Louise takes up the tale.

'Hello, Louise, what are you doing here?'

We were standing together on the steps of St. Andrew's Cathedral, Singapore, waiting for the previous service to finish, and I had recognised her immediately. She was Ann Phillips, who, as Ann Mott, had been at Oxford with Geoffrey and me and had married a chap now in the air force. Curiously enough Geof's parents had been close to the Motts in earlier years in the way academic families were, in the Oxford of the 1920s and '30s, and we had learned with some excitement how Ann, having got married to her Tony not long after us, had been able to join him by securing a passage on the British Airways flying boat service which then took about a week. But this was war time and I was away from home.

After a couple of weeks at Alor Gajah on my own, following Geof's mobilisation, I did my best to get things packed up for whatever eventuality, as the Japanese continued to press southward, but it was very lonely and I could see no future on my own. My nearest friends were at Tampin a few miles away, where Lester Simpson-Gray was District Officer and Mary, his wife, had been urging me to join them while there was a chance, as families were flooding South and she would inevitably have to find room for some.

17

It seemed the best thing to do in all the uncertainties, so I packed up our little Flying Standard 12 H.P. and, loaded down with Geof's trunk, my typewriter, sewing machine and gramophone, topped by a hen-coop and a broody hen, came to rest briefly at the D.O.'s rambling house a little way up the hill above the District Office itself.

The Simpson-Grays were kindness itself, but I really couldn't settle down or be particularly useful. The war situation was changing from day to day. Already the trickle of European families heading South from Perak and Selangor to the imagined safety of Singapore was becoming greater each day, and what was happening to Geof? I had actually received five letters from him written in pencil on what appeared to be loo-paper, in which he gave racy accounts of the early days of mobilisation. Then, to my surprise, I received a telegram sent, not by Geof but by his cousin, with instructions to come to Singapore at once where a room was booked at Raffles Hotel. This earth-shaking cable, together with another from Rosemary Peel, wife to John Peel in the Colonial Secretariat, entreating me to come down, finally clinched the matter for me. So, taking leave of the Simpson-Grays and my broody hen, I packed up the car once again and set out on Christmas Eve for a solo journey of some 150 miles to Singapore and safety. The mother hen made it, I later learned, and successfully hatched her brood of chicks!

It was now Christmas Day and I had walked across from the Raffles the few hundred yards to the Cathedral compound, intending to come to the 8 o'clock communion, when I had bumped into Ann Phillips.

'Well, Geof is with the Volunteers and I'm really looking for a job.'

In a few words, while the congregation filed out, Ann said she thought that stenographers were needed at General H.Q. where she herself was working, and why not come along?

So it was: a college friendship, a chance meeting, and I was on the road, the road which was to take me away from Geof, certainly, but to comparative safety and to a career I would never have dreamed of, through unimagined hazards. For three weeks I continued in my job, sufficiently stretched from day to day, but nevertheless with growing alarm at what was coming to be seen as a possible or rather an inevitable disaster, particularly in view of what had happened at Hong Kong. On that very day Hong Kong had fallen to the Japanese: what miracle could now save Singapore?

By now General Wavell was commander in chief, but he soon decided to move the headquarters to Java. It was a command with rapidly decreasing and failing forces, in particular in regard to aircraft, where the losses had been immense and the surviving machines no match for the Japanese Navy Zero fighters.

To pull things together Wavell aimed to concentrate his staff in the Dutch Netherlands Indies, bringing together allied representatives to form what was termed ABDACOM, based at the Dutch hill station of Lembang near Bandung. Time was running out and I was asked if I would go with the rest of the administrative staff of Air H.Q. and other H.Q. units which were being evacuated from the Island on a naval supply ship on the following day.

What was I to do? My heart told me to stay with Geof, but in a sensible talk that evening he pointed out that we certainly would not be able to help one another in the event of a surrender and, indeed, I would only be an anxiety. Moreover my best friend in the office, Beryl Stevenson, had decided to go.

CHAPTER 4

LAST DAYS

(Geoffrey resumes)

Like the promise made at our marriage service 'for better or worse' I chose to begin this saga with an account, in the Introduction, of that awful day when after eighteen months of relative bliss Louise I were parted by the circumstances of war. There was no time for grieving, no occasion for despair. Each of us had a job to do — mine was bound up with the Volunteers and the part they played in the larger Malayan scene, while Louise moved away in the safe hands of an allied headquarters' setup, albeit on foreign soil. Just as well that the future was hidden from us at that difficult moment of separation. I did have one or two letters from Louise in Java, but I must leave it to her to recount, in a later chapter, how things turned out for her.

What follows here is the story of my adventures covering the next three and a half years. It is based on a 'shorthand' diary which I was able to keep on scraps of paper during those POW days and which I wrote up in some detail during our seven week voyage from Australia to England in December 1945.

The Japanese invasion of Singapore Island on the 11th January abruptly brought to an end our days of static defence based on the Swimming Club. The next day our machine gun company was moved to the front line in the Northern suburbs of the town around Orange Grove Road. Very soon the Japanese had control of the water supply, mainly the McRitchie reservoir in the centre of the Island. The end, it would seem, could not be many days away. During those last queer days which now seem like the unrealities of a dream we were left pretty much to ourselves. We were quite close to the front line, but we did not see a single Japanese — not even one of the several snipers who pestered us continually. It was just watch and wait, cook and eat, clean the gun, report to Company Headquarters

*Wedding day: Fellows' Garden, Corpus Christi College, Oxford,
6th July 1940*

The author eating manggisteens beside the road leading from Kuala Kubu to the Gap Resthouse, Selangor, Malaya (2,200 ft.)
November 1941

and other matters of routine. I found it exciting to explore the houses round about, expecting to meet a Japanese sniper at every turn. I scrounged for any good supplies left behind in larders and fridges. I even had a bath and washed my overalls.

One thing I really disliked was being dive-bombed. A Jap plane comes circling round – no opposition of course – and it may well be trying to spot our position. I have taken cover behind a clump of bananas, hoping that a couple of concrete slabs might offer some protection against bullets. Round comes the plane again and whiz! down it dives apparently straight for our gun post. My moment of concentrated prayer coincides with a burst of machine gun fire from the plane. The wall of the next house is spattered with bullets and crash! the expected bomb demolishes the kitchen quarters of the house behind. We draw our breath freely again and can have our lunch in comparative peace!

We even had moments of fun on the very last day of hostilities although we knew that things were pretty bad. On the previous few nights darkness had been partially abolished by the awe-inspiring flames of burning oil dumps in different parts of the Island, and I can remember writing some hysterical notes and Last Words by their glare. We had been told that resistance would continue to the last, and for my part I fully expected to perish in the final hours preceding the fall of our much-vaunted fortress.

But surrender was the idea furthest from our thoughts when at 4 pm Judy O'Grady, my Company Commander, read out the declaration. How we hated the anticlimax of it all, and how we respected his being unable to restrain his disappointment and his tears. We threw down our arms in the appointed place, only to be told moments later that the terms had not been completed and that we were to fight on. With a cheer we grabbed the nearest rifle or whatever and returned to our lately abandoned position.

We were to expect enemy tanks, so we amused ourselves rehearsing how to time the throwing of grenades with the firing of the gun. I was stuck in a hole, recently dug for a prospective banana palm no doubt. It was handy for throwing a grenade to be sure, but apart from that the cover was minimal. The expected tanks however did not roar up and our suspense was brought to an end by the second and final order to surrender, which came when dusk had already fallen upon the scene.

That night there was much talk of escaping — not that it was a new idea, for several times in the previous days, and once or twice at Tanjong Rhu, Elliott had broached the subject and had proclaimed in no uncertain manner that he would not tolerate the life of a POW, but would attempt to escape at the earliest opportunity. He was our Section Commander, a queer fellow, about whom I will have much to say later on, and who attracted me considerably by his qualities of efficiency, leadership and keen sense of duty.

I had jokingly asked him whether he would take us all with him if he decided to go, but on that occasion he did not commit himself in any way. In the light of subsequent events it was clear that the people who went off on the night of the capitulation had the best chance of getting away: if we had put our idea of taking a yacht from the Singapore Yacht Club into effect we might have been successful, but we had thought of heading for Sumatra or Java, not India, and in that case, like so many other unfortunate people, we would probably have run straight into the main Japanese fleet. Anyhow, we decided to do nothing about it that night and the five of us on Elliott's gun slept peacefully like piglets in a row under a big tarpaulin on the lawn.

Monday the 16th February was spent by the remnant of 'A' Machine Gun Company in a spacious house somewhere near the Goodwood Park Hotel. A handful of loyal Malays had stayed with us to the end and these were heartbroken and even dissolved into tears when they were told to step out of their Volunteer uniform into sarongs and disappear: they wanted to share our captivity with us.

The example of these boys contrasted nobly with the behaviour of the majority of the Malays in the Company who silently and one by one vanished from the scene in the course of the last few days. I felt, for my part, that our failure to protect them was ample excuse for their desertion, and I had realised all along that the 'guru' is not necessarily the best type of man to make a good soldier.

On Tuesday the big march to Changi took place. The Imperial

22

Japanese Army had ordered that Singapore should be evacuated by 3.30 pm, as far as I can remember, and everyone was so scared of our captors that we scuttled out like a bunch of rabbits. The march was long and thirsty: Elliott and I were in the front of the column of Volunteers and we stuck together until about the ninth mile (it was some 15 miles altogether) when he got a lift on a crowded lorry. After a while I got a ride too, but did not meet up with him and the rest of our Company again until I arrived at Kitchener Barracks late in the evening. That night I slept between him and Padre Petter, who had done heroic work throughout the whole lamentable show. Lying on concrete was a novel experience.

Wednesday 18th February. Our captivity had properly begun. It was remarkable how early on the rock-bottom instincts of man began to assert themselves: everyone scrounged, thieved, jockeyed for positions, hoarded and overate with the utmost intensity and I at once felt heartily sick of the whole atmosphere. I refused to accumulate a vast quantity of rubbish which might or might not come in useful at a later date. I went down to the sea and had a wonderful swim. I talked at length with Elliott over the possibilities of making an escape. I ate slender meals and tried not to feel hungry. The weather was magnificent but hot, and because of the shortage of water everyone was terribly thirsty. Organisation so far was deplorable. Latrines, shallow and open, speedily became pestilential spots. It was obvious that, if these conditions endured, dysentery and other related diseases would ravage the encampment in no time.

On the Thursday our Company of the Volunteers moved to the top storey of another block of barracks where we had much more room. The view over the straits of Johore was superb. I appreciated the situation, but felt a kind of suppressed nervous excitement, engendered, I suppose, by the possibilities of escape which still engaged all Elliott's waking moments.

That morning he and I were on a fatigue carrying and storing masses of tinned goods in the old school buildings: he had asked several other Volunteers whether they would join him in an attempt to get off the Island — he wanted a party of five or six — and they had all disappointed him. He said he was determined to go accompanied or alone, but if I still wanted to come with him he would be very glad to have me. With a queer feeling inside me, the same, I think that I had experienced before going into Schools for my Finals, I said 'Yes', and knew then, from the demon of pride within, that there could be no turning back.

Our preparations were very simple: discard everything that was not absolutely essential, take the minimum of kit and iron rations, see that our waterbottles were full, and have two or three hours' sleep during the afternoon. We saw our C.O. who agreed not to record our names on any list given to the I.J.A., said goodbye to a few of our friends, and about an hour before dusk walked out of the barrack-block in a state of subdued inebriation arising from the thrill of anticipated freedom.

CHAPTER 5

VENTURE FOR FREEDOM

Escape: what utter fools the two of us were to attempt it! Blissfully confident in our state of comparative ignorance we had decided to make our break that very evening — it was only four days since the surrender had taken place — for, we reasoned, the sooner we went the easier it would be to walk out of the encampment unimpeded by wire or patrols, and the less likelihood there would be of organised Japanese policing of the Island.

The pity of the whole affair was that we were lamentably ill-provided for, in respect of drugs and money, and were without any sort of map either of Singapore or the mainland. We were so intent on the immediate prospect of escaping that we were not fully alive to the many weaknesses of our plans and preparations and there is no doubt that had I been less ignorant I would not have accepted Elliott's invitation so unhesitatingly. But at least let me say this: at the time I had absolutely no regrets, no qualms about the future, no fears of meeting an early death from Japanese sentry or by the more gloomy formality of a firing squad. Thoughts of Louise had been pushed into the background by the tremendous happenings of the past weeks, and it seems strange, but at this stage I was so conscious of the immense anti-climax, so out of tune with life by reason of the jarring note of bathos that sounded within me, that I scarcely seemed to care whether I survived or not.

It was uncomfortably hot as we walked up the Changi road with the warm evening sun on our backs. We were heavily clothed for the tropics — I had a shirt and shorts on underneath my overalls — and in addition our kit, consisting of haversack, waterbottle, and a respirator case crammed with our necessities slung in front in the 'alert' position, was altogether pretty heavy. I can well imagine that we presented a suspicious appearance as we approached the Military Police picket which, reinforced by a high-ranking officer, red tape and braid all over him, was stationed at the road junction by the Post Office. Where were we going? Oh, just trying to find our way to the Kitchener Barracks to join the main body of Volunteers. This glib lie carried us past the braid and the arm-bands and we soon branched off from the road down which they directed us and struck across the padang towards the confines of the camp.

I could make up a fine story of our get-away, crawling between Jap guards, running the gauntlet of rifle fire from a watchful patrol, hiding up to our necks in the stinking slush of the mangrove swamps — but no: truth compels me to state that our escape was the easiest that one could possibly imagine. We waited for dusk and ate our supper in the scrub by the edge of the swamps, listening to the sounds of community singing which came across from the Aussies in their barracks in Selarang. We made our way, cautiously enough, you can guess, through the area where we knew the Japanese were stationed, and simply walked straight out, quite hilarious with our new-found freedom.

The new moon, four or five days old, set early and we walked and stumbled and walked again in what Elliott judged to be the direction of Ponggol until well after midnight, when we halted in some rubber, celebrated our first night in freedom by munching some army biscuits and raisins, and laughing heartily together over our good luck and those Jap-happy people in Changi who were too scared of our captors to move a muscle or wink an eyelid without express permission. After that, sleep, in spite of mosquitoes, was sweet and cool, but all too short.

Dawn was already breaking up the shadows in the obscurity of the rubber when I silently woke Elliott, and at once we moved off to find a suitable spot for lying up during the day. We must have gone on, however, for well over an hour, through rubber and Chinese kampong, coming across plenty of signs of retreating fighting soldiers, and Japanese 'poached eggs' which had already made their appearance on the walls or over the doorways of every shack and shanty. These signs of local acquiescence in the enemy occupation made us most suspicious of trusting ourselves to any Chinese in these parts. When we eventually hid in some deep silt-pits in a rubber estate, after having seen more Malays than we liked, the morning was already far advanced. We ate, we slept.

I think that some children must have stumbled upon our unconscious figures, for I woke up to the sound of scampering feet on dry leaves and found to my dismay that a tin of bully had gone west. Obviously it was time to be off and away, and besides the sun was getting low; it was about an hour before sunset.

It was now that we had a spot of excitement. We came down unexpectedly on a major road linking the eastern part of the Island with Seletar and the Naval Base to the north, and we were not altogether surprised to observe that it seemed to be well patrolled by Japs passing and repassing in frequent lorries. It was a new sort of thrill to play hide and seek with fate, to dash across the road and hurl myself into the undergrowth while a lorry swept past packed with enemy troops.

How many miles we covered that night from dusk onwards I could not possibly estimate. But we were on our feet for a good eight or nine hours and must have zigzagged across a large section of the Changi-Ponggol area. Ponggol was our immediate goal, for this was the place on the Straits of Johore, well known to Elliott who had kept a yacht there in better days. The trouble was that he only knew where it was — not how to reach it from Changi, and as we had no maps we wasted many hours and much energy before we made it. That night is like a bad dream. I have memories of staggering through morasses up to my knees, of making repeated enquiries from every Chinese house we came to, of how, at one place late on in the night, a young Chinese boy touchingly offered us a candle to light us on our way, and how in despair at ever getting anywhere we struck boldly up the main road and walked slap through the village of Semerboh, cursing the kampong dogs for the noise they made. It was here that we nearly came unstuck for the first time. A little way out of the village the beam of a torch flashed out about 50 yards in front of us and made us dive hastily for the shelter of the drain.

A clinking of arms speedily brought it home to us that we had almost run into a Jap guard or block house, so we beat a quick retreat down the drain and got away by making a detour round the kampong. Again my memory of the exact sequence of events fails me, but it was at this point that I had the laugh over Elliott when he fell slap into a well – fortunately one of the shallow variety that the Malays use for bathing, so that he was only wet up to his middle.

The last thing I remember before we lay down to sleep in some rubber was passing by a leper colony. It must have been about three or four in the morning, but the subdued buzz of talk and movement showed that the place was still awake. A wave of intense pity and horror came over me as I peered into the dormitory and caught the smell of the offensive effluvia. We quickly turned away from that unhappy scene and hurried on, knowing now that Ponggol must be near at hand, with the crossing of the Straits of Johore the next big obstacle.

Within an hour or so of daylight, after walking through coconut palms and fishing kampongs, we were profoundly relieved to find ourselves on the outskirts of the village we had been searching for during the last three days. We lay up in the outbuildings of the first deserted bungalow we came across and had no difficulty in sleeping until dusk. Some Chinese however had obviously seen us take refuge, for when we emerged at dusk two Chinese lads came up and offered us packets of biscuits and some tins of baked beans (army rations!) and, what was more important to us, said they had a boat which, for a consideration, we could use to cross the Straits. This was almost too good to be true: surely there was some snag? But no. After more conversation in whispered broken Malay, we gathered that they really had a boat of some sort and wanted ten dollars for it. We swore we had no money and hoped that one of the youths would ferry us across, taking the boat back – and all for love! But catch a Chinese doing anything without making some profit out of the bargain. They had spotted Elliott's ring, a treasured possession given him by his father, and nothing could satisfy them but to have this in exchange for the boat. Reluctantly Elliott parted with the ring and the bargain was completed by our giving up a jar of Golden Shred marmalade, presumably to offset the biscuits and the beans.

The young crescent moon was still high in the sky when we left our hiding place and were led by the two Chinese across the mudflats to their boat. It was a yacht's dinghy, capable of holding six or seven people, and pretty heavy it was too as we dragged it over the mud to deep water. However it was marvellous to have our most extravagant hopes fulfilled with such ease: Elliott took the sculls and off we pushed for Johore and the north. The crossing itself was idyllic. Instead of having to swim the Straits as we had feared, to have a boat and such blissful conditions seemed to us a happy augury for the future.

It took us perhaps three quarters of an hour to cross that mile-wide stretch of water, paddling gently to avoid making splashes and creaking noises. But this would not have prevented us from being detected had there been any Jap vessel or lookout on the watch, for the brilliant moon striking low across the water must have made us visible from a long way off.

We had plenty of time to enjoy the magic of the scene: it was a Malayan night of the very best, calm and mild with the constellations and Milky Way blazing out as the moon sank down. What entranced me most, however, was the phosphorescence in the water: each time you dipped the paddle you stirred up a cauldron of molten silver and gold, and drops of liquid light fell from the blade. Elliott said it surpassed anything he had seen in his five years' experience of sailing in these waters. The only lurid touch which brought us back to reality was the glare from the still-burning Naval Base: this was five or six miles away and the huge fire from time to time sent up colossal pillars of flame which momentarily lit up the hills round about. We tied up to a mangrove root, ate some raisins and biscuits, speculated on our good fortune up to the present and then, for my part, quickly fell asleep on the floorboards.

Sunday 22nd February. I awoke as the first glimmers of dawn were casting grey light on the sheltered waters of the Straits now so wonderfully behind us and together we dragged the boat up into the cover of the mangroves. Again, what luck! Instead of making our landing in the middle of a mangrove swamp and miles from any habitation, as Elliott had expected, we found ourselves, after a few paces inland, near a small kampong, a Chinese fishing village.

We approached a weatherbeaten fisherman: could he tell us

perhaps how to get to Kota Tinggi and how far it was? Oh, it was far, twenty miles maybe, but it would not be safe for us to journey by day. No, we agreed: perhaps we could hide somewhere and go on our way at nightfall? Yes, there was a fowl house just over there: we could lie up in it during the day; we would be quite safe. This was good enough for us. We picked up a young coconut and found a cleanish piece of cement in one part of the fowl house where we sat and drank the juice. I then raked up some old boards and dozed serenely till late afternoon.

It is high time that I introduced you to Elliott, my only companion for the next few weeks. He was a one-striper like me, and had been No 1 of our Machine Gun Section during those last four hectic days in Singapore. Ever since I had begun to get to know him in Tanjong Rhu in the early days of January, I had been considerably impressed by his personality: in fact I was overjoyed when he chose me to be No 4 on his gun. He was twenty-six but older than his years, having grown up to learn independence early. He claimed that he had eloped at the age of sixteen with the girl who was still engaged to him, and had the nerve to expect his parents to accept the fait accompli, permit the marriage and give him an allowance of £1,000 per year — which apparently his father was then in a position to do. But the parents were unyielding and Bob remained bachelor and penniless while the beautiful Elaine in due course became private secretary to one of the big shots in the Government of South Africa.

Elliott's father, a retired major with a distinguished record of army service, had decided that Bob should also go into the army, and nearly cut him off with a shilling when he flatly refused. The blitz blew over however when Bob left King's College School, Wimbledon to study medicine at London University. He was there for only eighteen months; Major Elliott went broke; there was a younger son still to be educated. So that was when Bob came out to Singapore with a job in the Mercantile Bank.

All went well for a while and he enjoyed the life, but his luck did not last. As far as I could make out Elliott was made a scapegoat by the Bank in a case involving some financial scandal. With a view to recovering the initiative and establishing his innocence, he had planned to break into the bank building and abstract an important document which had been suppressed. A confidant turned informer, and Elliott was caught red-handed as he was climbing the drainpipe. The subsequent court case lasted months. Elliott defended himself personally, taking his case to the Court of Appeal, but to no avail and in the event he went to Changi Gaol to serve a month's sentence.

During these long-drawn-out proceedings he was living on his capital and he came out of prison in 1939 with very few dollars to his name. In addition practically all his European friends had dropped him; he was to all intents and purposes a social outcast. But this did not worry him. From early on he had always been more interested in the Chinese, and when he was in the Bank he had plenty of chances of making friends among them. It was a matter of no account to them if a man happened to have been in prison, and they proved loyal to Elliott through thick and thin. Many a time he would have gone hungry but for their hospitality; at times he was living on about twenty dollars a month. But Elliott is first and foremost a fighter, and by hook and crook he was soon making a living for himself. He was far too independent ever to take employment under anyone; he preferred to be his own master. Eventually he set up a business as a chemical engineer in partnership with an astute Chinese, and was doing well in a number of lines of manufactured articles and products in the chillie sauce and disinfectant line until the war broke out.

Perhaps you can gather from this bald account of my companion's career (as retailed by himself, I hasten to explain) something of the nature of his character. His cynicism and extreme independence make him quite careless about other people; he is not a social creature, and apart from one or two intimate friends he only cultivates people as long as they are of use to him. I had better say that it was only gradually that I came to know Elliott properly: during our first few days together we talked little, but after the first week or so of our escape, when the initial strain and excitement had slackened, we began to have long conversations together as we walked along or lay up in the jungle.

31

The plan which Elliott had conceived was pretty fantastic, for apart from the first stage across the Straits he knew nothing of the conditions of the country across which he proposed we should go. I gaily acquiesced, being quite content to leave everything to him, for I knew even less and was quite prepared to go on trudging from day to day, risking death from a Jap's rifle or from malaria, and not worrying about the possibility or otherwise of eventually reaching the coast of Province Wellesley opposite Penang, securing a boat and sailing to Ceylon or India. The idea of going so far north was that by so doing we would miss the northern tip of Sumatra, with the north-east monsoon behind us; and to succeed, our adventure would have to be concluded by about 15th May, when the south-west monsoon breaks, but this I did not know until later. The distance from Singapore to Penang, by the way, is about 420 miles. How on earth would we replace our boots?

Elliott had been knocking about Malaya, Siam and Borneo for three or four years and had never once caught fever. I think he must have been extremely lucky, though in considering our equipment he underrated the danger of our getting malaria in the course of our trip. In his travels he had mainly been in big jungle where malarial mosquitoes do not necessarily breed, and he did not realise that much of our way was to be through or along the edge of rubber estates, that these estates would not be controlled any longer and that we would be travelling during the bad malarial months of the year. Malaria did in fact prove to be our undoing and we later cursed ourselves time and again for not having laid in stocks of quinine. But in other ways we were not so badly off, seeing that we had to scrounge everything beforehand as best we could. Elliott wore tunic, riding breeches, long puttees and hosetops over his boots, while I had a set of overalls with short puttees and hosetops. Underneath I wore an aertex shirt and pants and khaki shorts, mighty hot by day, and by night too when we were walking hard, but I never regretted carrying such an excess of clothing when it came to sleeping on cold, damp ground in the bitterly chill small hours.

In other ways our equipment was the same: haversack and gas-mask case stuffed with essential items and iron rations – tin of bully beef, condensed milk and sardines each. But we often carried pounds of other foodstuffs like rice, sugar, sweet potatoes or tapioca root which we either thieved or were given from time to time. One thing of immense importance: we always had plenty of matches, for helpful friends used to press these on us. Last but quite vital was the prismatic compass which Elliott had successfully concealed on his person after the surrender. We certainly could not have gone far without it.

CHAPTER 6

JUNGLE FRINGE

Our first Sunday on the mainland of Johore ended as pleasantly as it had begun. We were undisturbed during the day, and at dusk Jo Hok, our friendly fisherman, did us proud by bringing us each a plate of rice and some pieces of meat which tasted to me like chicken: Elliott thought it might be fruit-bat (kluang). It was delicious. While we ate it Jo Hok politely sat apart (observe the innate courtesy of the Chinese) and then took us half a mile on our way towards Kota Tinggi. In the next three or four hours we put a good distance between us and the Straits; walking through rubber estates on roads which happily led always in the right direction we were able to swing along at a great pace. We crossed the Masai road at the seventeenth milestone, i.e. from Johore Bahru, and slept in the rubber on the further side of the road.

23rd February. One of the first thoughts of the day was usually: 'Where are we going to get breakfast?' and on this occasion we did not do too badly. Beyond this stretch of rubber we found a deserted Chinese house, quite a poor one. It had been ransacked thoroughly and there were signs of British troops there – tin hats, equipment and so on. We ransacked again, you may be sure, and collected a few pounds of rice and a tinful of sugar. I tried my hand at cooking some of the rice and made an awful glutinous mess of it: it was edible all right, and with some boiled papayas, also scrounged nearby, we had quite a satisfying meal. Perhaps it is significant, however, that in future Elliott usually did the cooking of the rice!

The previous days had been hard going, especially at night when we inevitably stumbled about a lot, and at the outset we had not been at all in good training. And did we sweat our guts out? Judging by the stink of our clothes we got rid of a lot of unnecessary fat and dirt – I speak for myself, of course. So you may guess how welcome was the good bath which we had in a stream in this same estate. We

34

stopped there for a few hours and washed all our clothes. It must have been about 3 pm when we pushed off again in a northerly direction, and the course we took involved crossing numbers of ravines which were very trying, considering the weight of all our baggage.

An hour or so before dusk we met five Chinese, refugees from Kulai, and soon made friends with them. They agreed to help us on our way at nightfall, so we retired meanwhile to the jungle which bordered the rubber. They gave us two young coconuts, the water like nectar, and at dusk went away to fetch us some food from friends of theirs who were camping out in the jungle not far off. We were delighted at the contents of the tiffin-carrier: rice, pork and salt; we rarely failed to enjoy any grub we got on the trek! One of these lads had been a taxi-driver and knew the main roads in Johore; from him we got some useful (and some misleading) information about places and distances, from which I later made a rough sketch of the country we hoped to cross.

They were touchingly kind and the taxi-driver insisted on giving me a tiny pot of 'Tiger Balm', a panacea known throughout Malaya: Elliott said there was precious little to it but resin in a petroleum jelly base, but you could use it as a liniment all right and it proved really helpful afterwards when Elliott had a cold. The Chinese said you could even eat the stuff if you had a belly-ache!

That night, after hours of weary walking and stumbling through the vegetation that the rubber estates use as a cover-crop, we ended up dog-tired at a Chinese refugee kongsi where we were received quite enthusiastically by the people. They were all up, and indeed we always found that the Chinese sat about chatting well on into the night. They hastened to make up the fire, boil a kettle and prepare hot sweetened milk. I lapped it up – it was so good and refreshing – and between sips told our story to our eager hosts. They were very keen to hear about the fall of Singapore and their weatherbeaten faces in the flickering firelight made an animated scene. As for the capitulation, you can imagine that I was hard put to explain it away!

24th February. We slept for the remainder of that night in the scrub near the kongsi. Soon after dawn I was woken by one of the

Chinese who said they were all returning to their homes that very morning and were starting at once. He gave me directions as to our route and also a tin of rice-flour. This we mixed with water and sugar: it did not make very appetising fare.

We emerged that afternoon at about 4 pm and before long found a Chinese hut whose occupant gave us a meal and then, after consultation with various neighbours, set us on our way for a mile or so. Towards dusk we crossed the Keng-Keng road at the thirteenth milestone and then the directions we had been given failed us. Time after time this happened until we were forced to realise that the Chinese (or Asiatic in general) has a most illogical mind which is incapable of giving precise directions. Distances especially are of little concern to him and eventually we placed little faith in such estimates. On this occasion, anyhow, when I am sure we wandered off the right track — the simplest thing in the world to do, with the tricky moonlight filtering through the rubber — we did not do so badly, for we hit on a Chinese kongsi of very frightened Hokkiens.

There were fifteen or twenty of them in the usual sort of plank and atap dwelling and at first they did not want to have anything to do with us, but they thawed sufficiently to brew us the most wonderful coffee; they also offered chunks of boiled tapioca root which I tasted for the first time; it made good chewing and was sweetish in flavour. We did not stay long as our hosts obviously wanted us out of the way, and as soon as we had finished one of them led us out, past the piggeries and the vegetable garden back into the rubber and showed us a path to follow.

Our next landfall was a Chinese refugee kongsi of women and children, and my goodness! what a scene we stirred up by our arrival. As usual I approached first and cautiously called out at the doorway that we were friends and that they were not to be afraid. I was a bit nonplussed by rushings and scufflings that followed: forms emerged dimly from mosquito nets and fled into the background; babies started wailing. Then a jittery man appeared and I tried to explain what we wanted: directions and food. I did not think we would have much luck with this nervous individual, but he gave us bubor (rice-porridge) and sugar and did us an even better turn in his desire to clear us out of his vicinity, by leading us to a group of woodcutters about a quarter mile away.

Our jitterbug knocked them up and after some talk found one who was willing to guide us to the big jungle on the further side of the Kota Tinggi road. This was grand, but we did not know what we were in for. It must have been getting on for midnight when we set off: we made one false start through a small patch of jungle and then away we went, walking on and on, along endless tracks which wound over barren undulating country once covered by pineapple plantations. The stars were brilliant; the moon set, and still we continued. Would this night march go on for ever? I kept one eye on the Great Bear (Orion soon sank below the horizon) and saw we were going mainly in a north-westerly direction. Elliott and I were careful to remonstrate with our guide when he tried to go off at a tangent at every crossroads.

We must have done twelve miles or more across this waste pineapple country before we cut the Kota Tinggi road at the sixteenth milestone from Johore Bahru, and even then our guide refused to leave us although we were dead with fatigue and only longed to find a good spot and sleep. He wanted to make sure that we were on the right road to the next woodcutters' kongsi and all our entreaties and curses would not deter him. Nam Yek pineapple estate: that was the place he wanted. We arrived at the main gate, went in and dismissed him with words and gestures of repeated thanks, but we had not gone more than a few yards when he turned back and called to us.

I groaned afresh and cursed the old blighter. This was not the right way, he said, and plucked at my sleeve pulling me along with him. I was too tired to resist, so back to the main road we went and after another mile, maybe less, we turned in at another road into the estate. At last our guide was satisfied. This was the road to the woodcutters. The stars were already beginning to pale in the east when we said goodbye to the old Chinese; I realised how little he had deserved our curses and gave him a box of matches as a token of our debt to him.

25th February. On towards the jungle at the crack of dawn. In spite of our tiredness we had to make as fast as we could for the line of trees just visible beyond the acres of pineapples, and the track we followed offered no cover at all. Two Chinese on cycles alarmed us by saying that Japanese were coming up behind, so we jumped into the pineapples, never mind how dewy and prickly they were, and sneaked over the crest of the hill. Our apprehensiveness rather spoiled my enjoyment of the beauties of the morning: the marvellous long shadows in the hollows and the mists rising over the hills. But however hard we scanned the road for signs of Jap cyclists or lorries we saw nothing, and concluded that the two Chinese had seen a convoy coming along the Kota Tinggi road and had straightaway taken fright and made tracks for home.

By now the sun was getting up and we were hot; we plucked a couple of nice pineapples and were grateful that providence had supplied us with this timely breakfast. We came upon a poor Chinese dwelling and were invited with charming courtesy to share their meal. We sat down to a little square table with a young Chinese who in his simple garb looked like a Buddhist novice except that he had no tonsure. His father politely took his rice outside while the young wife quietly went about her duties, her baby on her hip. We ate beautiful rice and stewed pig's liver, exchanging odd words and smiles with our charming host. What a happy interlude!

From here the jungle was not far and we lay up at the edge for the day, first disposing of several pineapples. I learned for the first time that too many pineapples means too many sore mouths!

At about 4 pm, after a most refreshing sleep we came out and had another feed at a nearby kongsi. The people here put us in touch with an English-speaking Chinese who, however, was not much help in giving us directions or news, but they showed us the way to a woodcutters' kongsi some two miles away, at the jungle edge in the direction we wanted to go, so off we pushed and arrived there soon after dusk. And what a reception we had! Once the Chinese realised who we were and that we were not marauding Japanese, they surrounded us in scores, brought us into one of their dwellings, sat us down, lit candles, gave us hot water to drink and plied us with a flood of questions while rice was being cooked. I was quite overwhelmed by this display of enthusiasm and hospitality and could

38

not help comparing the simple open-handed generosity of these people with the niggardliness of our own kind. All these Chinese knew they would be taken and killed if it became known that they had received us, and yet that did not influence them in the least. They really were fine people.

As usual we tried to find out as much as we could about the way ahead and the direction of the various towns and villages in the neighbourhood. One bright spark suggested we should climb a high hill which was not far off, from which we could see everywhere. This seemed an odd thing to do at night, but we fell in with this and at about 10 pm, after a grand meal, a procession of some eight or ten of us set off along twisting jungle paths, sometimes negotiating tricky parts where there was no path at all. The moon was full, but to help us over the snags and pitfalls the Chinese had electric torches.

It was a fantastic climb. After an hour's exhausting scrambling we reached the summit and after the last part of the ascent, steep and slippery in the extreme, with plenty of thorn-trees to make it nastier still, I practically collapsed. I had thought I was in fairly good training but this test showed me up, although it must be remembered that our kit and haversacks were quite heavy.

The view from the top was most impressive: the trees and scrub had been cleared and we could see the jungle rolling away below us in all directions. In the moonlight the hills by Renggam and Kota Tinggi were clearly outlined. It was altogether a superb panorama. Elliott took bearings, then after bidding our Chinese friends farewell we lay down to sleep in a little shelter that had been built by the owner of Nam Yek estate. In the cool pure air of that altitude we slept well and soundly.

26th February. The dawn which we witnessed from the top of our hill was indeed lovely and is one of the most enchanting memories of our trek. Below us was a sea of mist, broken in patches where trees standing on higher ground pushed through their heads, and beyond, the heights of Renggam and Kota Tinggi raised themselves grandly above the rolling vapour which however soon obscured everything as it rose in the growing heat of the early sun.

We munched some dry biscuits and then plunged down the steep slopes. For half an hour or so we toiled through the most trying jungle where thorny palms tore at our hands and clothes and we wondered if this was to continue until we reached the further edge which might be five or fifteen miles distant. But again luck was with us. We came out on to a path, probably opened up by woodcutters, which led gently down towards Kulai, and so we were able to make good progress in spite of being very thirsty.

The beauty of all this was suddenly marred: I remarked to Elliott that a strange smell hung on the air, a sickly sweet odour that became more and more nauseating. It was explained when we came upon two corpses lying on their faces by the side of the path, the flesh already decomposed leaving the skin drawn taut over the bones. These were the remains of two Malays, policemen of the Johore Forces, around whom were scattered their various belongings carelessly tipped out of their suitcases. We rifled these again and came away the richer by a belt apiece, some buttons and one or two other oddments.

A couple of hundred yards further down we found three more skeletons, apparently of a woman and two lads, judging from their clothing which hung round them in shreds and other pieces of clothing which were strewn about. Their fate remained a mystery, and we could only conjecture that they were runaways or refugees: they might have met their end by starvation, or have been shot down in their flight. In any case we were only too glad to quit this valley of death and came out of the jungle at 3 pm, near a refugee kongsi. We got a meal of badly cooked rice and sugar and then lay up, resting on the fringe of the forest. It was here that Elliott became communicative for the first time and confessed that his real goal was South Africa and the beautiful Elaine!

At dusk we pushed on as usual, keeping the jungle on our right and after several hours' uneventful going through rubber lay down to sleep very tired indeed, but fairly pleased with the progress we had made.

27th February. We awoke to find ourselves near the edge of a pineapple estate in which we could see plenty of Chinese dwellings. So we tried the nearest one. The occupants were not yet astir, and it was only after repeated knocks and assurances that we were friends that the door was opened. A good-looking young Chinese greeted us, rather frightened at óur presence, but he said he would bring us food if only we would retire to the edge of the jungle. This, of course, we were only too eager to do and, sure enough, before very long our new friend returned with two neat packets of rice done up in banana leaves. This was steaming hot and delicious, for on top of each helping of rice was a fried egg and some salted soya beans which made the rice ten times more interesting.

The Chinese stayed and chatted with us for some while. He spoke excellent English and told us he had been a Johore Customs officer at Kulai until the tide of war had swept away his job and broken up his home. So here he was with his family of three (one child had recently died) and one or two other dependents, living as refugees on this estate. He was growing some vegetables but life was hard with so many mouths to feed and rice only obtainable at an exorbitant price. He had been impressed by the Japanese to do forced labour, and only managed to escape by appealing to the kindness of a Japanese officer who understood English.

Among other items of news he told us that Sumatra had already fallen. This was important news to us, as it meant that it was of no use considering Sumatra as a possible objective if we managed to get hold of a boat. We then questioned him about what was our best way towards Renggam and he told us the names of the villages which lay near our route and the distances between them. Much of his information was wrong, but heaven knows we were only too grateful for meeting such an intelligent and intelligible being and we could forgive a lot for the food he gave us.

At evening he again brought us some rice and then, under the stars, we set off across the acres of pineapples. We had not been walking very long when the compass showed that it disagreed with the path we had been given. Once again we asked some Chinese for help but in this case they were most reluctant. Eventually however, after much persuasion, one volunteered to show the way. He set off at a terrific pace and we followed breathlessly for half a mile or so, winding through the pineapples past many little Chinese dwellings

41

from which the occupants stared at such unusual apparitions.

When we were left to pursue our way alone, luck favoured us, as it had consistently done to date, and we came out of the estate by a Chinese woodcutters' kongsi. The men were sitting outside smoking their pipes and chatting together in the moonlight and they hailed us in a most friendly manner as we passed by. So we stopped and exchanged news. They gave us coffee to drink and also a quantity of toasted rice which, they assured us, would keep for some time, and after half an hour we continued on our way, finally lying down to sleep in a patch of jungle through which our track ran.

28th February. We had entered a region of small-holdings of rubber with bits of jungle and scrub in between: this lay at the edge of the jungle proper to the east of the railway line running from Kulai north towards Layang-Layang, roughly parallel to the direction we were taking. The day proved quite an eventful one and we covered a fair amount of ground as we were far enough away from the centres of civilisation to move by daylight without the risk of running into Japanese. It was pleasant, almost agreeable, to be walking along secluded tracks in the freshness of the dewy morning, with the sun coming over the tree-tops. It was on mornings such as this that I always felt inclined to burst into song or hymn and thank God for being alive, and for being so wonderfully preserved in our journeyings.

We had not been walking long when we came upon the hut of a poor Chinese, situated in the middle of one of the small rubber plots which I have mentioned: the whole area cannot have been more than four or five acres. The occupant was busy picking the quills off a porcupine which he told us he had just snared in the belukar with a rabbit snare. He showed us how he set it, pegging it to the ground. We would very much have liked to have shared in the repast, but he looked so very poorly off that we refrained, and contented ourselves by asking for drinking water. This he boiled for us, so we filled our bottles, had a drink and pushed off in the direction he told us towards Poliseng, our next immediate objective. During the next hour I remember having an animated discussion with Elliott on the English Educational system. We agreed on most things, but he was dogmatic in his views.

For breakfast we stopped at the first house we came to, one of a number of Chinese dwellings in this neighbourhood. The good wife, a buxom dame with two or three children hanging about, received us most kindly and gave us an excellent meal, rice with long beans and dried salt fish. How we relished such tasty dishes! She also gave us a needle and thread which we asked for. When we departed, repeatedly thanking her for her kindness (she knew only a few words of Malay), she called her husband who said he would guide us on our way past Poliseng, a small village of Chinese, where I noticed a couple of small cars, derelict presumably through lack of petrol. We did not stop but passed by the backs of the houses, from which women at their work gazed curiously at us, and soon our guide turned back after giving us further directions.

It must have been midday, and I remember how hot it was as we trudged along with our heavy packs. We fell in with another Chinese who, we gathered, was going to the same kongsi to which our first Chinese had directed us. This suited us well, for when we duly arrived there he introduced us and saved us a lot of trouble. This place was a kongsi for a rubber estate, and was quite a big one, well provided with all the necessities of life. We were given a grand meal with coffee, and on parting were pressed to take a tin of condensed milk by our enthusiastic host. But we refused with many thanks, telling him to give it to his children.

For some days now we had been concerned about our boots which were already showing signs of serious wear. Elliott had an idea to make galoshes out of sheet rubber, which might protect the soles and prolong their life. At this kongsi we noticed some old sheets hanging up and we begged a couple. Later in the afternoon we cut these up, shaping the rubber roughly to the size of our boots and discarding the rest.

Soon after this we stopped at another shack to enquire about our way but got little satisfaction as the two occupants turned out to be opium addicts, who having only recently come to this refuge could give us no adequate directions. They complained that they had nearly run out of chandu (untreated opium) and while we were there

43

they poured hot water on the dregs that remained in a bottle and drank the mixture up.

At the kongsi where we had stopped for lunch we had been told that we would have to cross a river before long, and although the opium addicts could tell us little else they did show us a path which apparently led in the right direction. We hastened off through secondary jungle where the mosquitoes were really bad and soon reached another Chinese hut in the middle of the usual patch of rubber. An aged Chinese told us the way — there was no one else in the hut — but said that the river was some way off, and if we liked we could stay overnight in his place. But Elliott did not like the look of the shack and I could not help shuddering when he told me he thought the man showed the signs of incipient leprosy.

The river proved to be only about half an hour's march away, but it was not pleasant going as the path curled and twisted among giant trees, and the roots projecting above the mud in huge folds tripped us up frequently.

The river was far from being a trickle. Indeed it was between forty and fifty feet across and flowed with a deep but subdued current. On our side the bank sloped down into the water, and very mucky it was. On the other the bank was steep and some rudely constructed wooden steps, like the end of a jetty, led out of the water. There was no alternative but to take off all our clothes and wade or if necessary swim across with our belongings held above our heads.

I was just taking off my boots and had been horrified at making my first acquaintance with leeches, one of which was well attached through my hosetop, when I made the far more alarming discovery that my precious sheath-knife was missing from the sheath at my belt. To lose one's knife on a jungle trek is a terrible calamity and for a moment I was dumbfounded. Then it struck me that I had taken it out at the spot where we had stopped to cut up the rubber sheets, and that it must still be there — as long as no one else had picked it up in the intervening two or three hours. By Elliott's watch it was now twenty to six. If I ran all the way I reckoned I would get to the spot in full daylight: I would almost certainly have to find my way back in the gathering dusk.

44

I shed all my garments except shirt and shorts, keeping my boots on of course, and ran back as fast as the difficult nature of the path would allow. I skirted the leper's house and bypassed the opium-addicts' dwelling, sticking a latex cup on an upright stick to mark the turn, in case it should be dark when I came back, and then sped on with hope and fear for the finding or loss of my knife clutching at my heart. Oh, what joy to see its blade glinting up at me by the side of the path! My relief was tremendous, and moreover I had done the trip much more quickly than I had anticipated. I could not have been more than about thirty-five minutes on that lap, I calculated.

With still half an hour of daylight in front of me I felt quite confident, although Elliott had said he would light a fire and wait at least twenty-four hours in case I got lost. In addition I had my whistle which might help me to find my way to him. The latex cup pointed my way and before long I was back at the leper's house. He asked me if I had found my knife (he had previously enquired the reason for my returning) and I was glad to say 'sudah dapat', I had. For the remainder of the way I had to go carefully; the jungle trees shut out the light and, although I never missed the path, I was afraid I might do so very easily. The fireflies were already about by the time I saw a strip of sky appear, and the river at my feet in the twilight.

I shouted the good news to Elliott (I could not see him on the further side) and he replied 'good work', adding that he had not expected me back so soon. He had waded across with his knife in his mouth — in case of crocodiles — and found that he had to swim only for a few yards, and while I had been away had made fifteen trips to and fro, getting all the barang across. He had not made a fire because of the difficulty of finding dry stuff just there and he had only had time to dry and clothe himself and have a snack of biscuits and raisins before I turned up. I quickly got out of my clothing, with some trepidation, I confess, because of the scare of leeches, and took my boots and clothes across in two trips: Elliott had done all the rest. I told him how everything had gone while I munched the last of the Army biscuits and, soon after, curled up happily on my groundsheet under a brilliant Malayan night, fell sound asleep.

CHAPTER 7

A BRUSH WITH THE ENEMY

Sunday 1st March. I awoke feeling fresh and gay and full of joie de vivre. By way of celebrating the new month I had a face wash and also brushed my teeth (a thing I rarely did, I regret). I had no soap, it is true, but I had the messy remains of a tube of toothpaste and a brush, relics from peace-time days. Elliott was a little tardy, so while he finished dressing I said I would scout on ahead: I felt sure that there were habitations not far off where we might get some breakfast.

The path led gently up from the river and in a couple of hundred yards I came upon a group of ramshackle dwellings, deserted, to my disappointment. However I continued along the path, which soon led into a small rubber holding and, sure enough, in the middle was a small hut with three Chinese at their breakfast.

I knocked and introduced myself: naturally they were a bit taken aback at the apparition but when I told them that there was only one other besides me, and all we wanted was some food, they became quite friendly and said it would be all right. In due course I returned with Elliott and we had a meal — bubor, as far as I can remember, the sloppy 'rice porridge' which is the usual breakfast dish of the poor, and although I ate it quite cheerfully Elliott said he could not stand the stuff.

Neither of us was equipped with any implement of attack (apart from our sheath knives) or for cutting our way through jungle or undergrowth, and we had been hoping to get hold of a parang sooner or later. In this dwelling Elliott noticed a good-sized parang, and took it up to examine it. It was just what we wanted, heavy enough to be useful in thick jungle, of good quality steel and well tempered. We bargained with the Chinese, offered three dollars, and the coveted weapon was ours.

Two hours later we were quite ready for another meal which we had at another humble Chinese shack, and not long after leaving this place we had an amusing experience at a large Chinese kongsi we came to. We were being regaled with tea and bananas and plied with innumerable questions when a certain Chinese joined the group. He was quite obviously a bit above the rest and we wondered who he might be when he invited us to his house which he said was quite near. This proved to be a wonderful affair, a veritable palace in the midst of Johore's jungle, a quaint and attractive mixture of Chinese and Malay architecture.

It was built around a courtyard and had the high-pitched, thatched roof of the Malay, with Chinese curling roof-ends and fancywork, decorated in Chinese taste and colour. Our delight and surprise at such a lovely place was increased by amusement when Ah Boon told us that for many years he had been a 'kuki' and 'boy' to various Europeans in Singapore, and the 'surats' (references) that he showed us were signed by people who were known to Elliott! We asked him why he had retired and he explained simply that his mother had called him back and so he had returned to his village and built this mansion in the 'ulu' (hinterland). He had a good amount of land round about on which he grew fruit and vegetables besides rubber and in fact in every way he seemed quite the country squire, lord of the neighbourhood, even down to the numerous household of relatives and hangers-on which he had to support.

He made the most perfect coffee that I have ever tasted, and we had several cups, with biscuits ad lib. We were most sorry to quit this pleasant haven, but how could we dally when there remained so many miles of the peninsula to traverse? And after all ours was an attempt to make our way out of the country and not a holiday trip, as kept on appearing to me. That night we bivouacked in a small deserted rubber holding and felt secure enough to build a roaring fire against the stump of an old tree.

On the 2nd March we nearly came unstuck. Our path lay toward the village of Layang-Layang: a good path too, far bigger and better than the ones we had hitherto been tracing. The goodwife of the humble shack where we breakfasted rather late in the morning had put us on to this path, and we followed it for maybe a mile or more when there opened before us a fine clearing, recently done, of many acres. On this were numerous atap huts, including some larger ones which were obviously Chinese.

We approached one of these kongsis in search of news, whereabouts of the Japanese and directions, as we were wont, and after causing some initial alarm to the inmates were reluctantly admitted. They were in a state of great nervousness, two women and a man who absolutely twittered with fear. They told us that the Japs came daily in search of provisions, that they had not been that morning but might appear on the scene at any moment: they would arrive at any odd hour, generally coming in twos and threes on bicycles.

Clearly this was not the best place for two runaways like us to delay in, so we pulled out at once, only too anxious to cease embarrassing these Chinese. So after retracing our steps for a few hundred yards we entered another kongsi to ask the way, for we felt we must have missed the right turn to the 'oil palm estate' to which the young Chinese customs fellow had directed us some days before. An old man kindly walked the short distance back to the main track to give us directions, when at that moment up came a young coolie carrying two small sacks of rice balanced on the usual kandar stick.

'This lad will show you the way,' our friend said. 'He is going in the same direction as you.'

Glad to have this guide we pushed off at a good pace, the coolie trotting easily ahead.

We cannot have continued like this for more than a few minutes when I heard an unusual sound behind me – I was following Elliott – and turned to see Japanese soldiers on cycles riding down the track towards us some 40 yards away. I know I instinctively uttered some warning sound and Elliott cried: 'Quick, in to the right,' but the recollection of what followed is a blurred memory of frantically tearing our way through dense high bracken, maddeningly obstructive, with shots popping behind us. I lost my cocky forage cap in a moment and was repeatedly hurled to the ground by numerous tendrils. I got a scratch over one eye and was absolutely winded.

Elliott and I had diverged slightly but now I joined him, the shooting having subsided, and we had a hasty and agonised council of war. This was our first brush with the Japanese and we did not like it at all, unarmed as we were. We did not know what steps they might take to hunt us down, but anyhow, when we had recovered our breaths and had a gulp of water, we made a half circuit to the left with the intention of throwing the Japs off our line of flight. The stratagem, such as it was, apparently worked, for that was the last we heard of our pursuers. I guess they were probably diverted by the young Chinese, who must have been taken, alas.

We were safe enough for the time being and took a much-needed rest for a few minutes in a patch of belukar, discussing what the Japs might do and what course we might best follow. We agreed we should quit the neighbourhood as fast as we could and make our way out to the north-west. Soon we got into jungle proper, where suitable paths helped us for a while, but this convenient way of proceeding did not last long and when we found ourselves floundering in the outskirts of a swamp we wondered if we had escaped from the frying-pan only to fall into the fire.

This particular swamp was typical of its kind. Not only was the jungle very thick, trees and shrubs growing in a morass, knee or thigh-deep, but full of an extremely prickly species of palm which hindered us continually. You can imagine how hard the going was, but we had no alternative but to press on as best we could, on a compass bearing, taking turns to go in front and hack our way through creeper and thorny palm.

We tried to make our way by stepping from tree to tree, but often we would plunge into the muck and almost lose our boots in the effort to get out. Elliott would consult the compass every few minutes and before long we grew exhausted and despondent. Elliott recalled an experience of his in Borneo when, as a result of a faulty compass, he had wandered around in a swamp for a week before he got out. We could not guess how far this jungle morass might stretch. The prospect was pretty dreary as rain had been falling steadily for some time and we were soaked through: moreover it appeared to be getting dark. We were wondering whether we might have to spend the night in this unutterable place when the ground suddenly appeared to be getting slightly drier and firmer. Soon there was no doubt: the ground rose steadily, and with thankful hearts we got out of the swamp to find ourselves on the edge of a clearing similar to the one we had left behind.

There was not more than half an hour of daylight left, so we hurriedly skirted the clearing in the hopes of finding some habitation, and perhaps food and help. Smoke was visible and before long the usual type of Chinese squatters' huts came into sight. But what an unpleasant reception we got! At one place an elderly Chinese rushed out in a frenzy and told us to get out, to go into the jungle; we could not stop an instant here. I was amazed, but it could have been as a result of the brush we had had earlier in the day. Heaven knows what awful reprisals might have taken place. I noticed several men standing by were casting hostile glances at us. One man thrust a handful of sweet potatoes at me and told us to get into the jungle and indicated the direction. To remain was impossible. As we turned to enter the jungle verge again I noticed that a splendid flaming sunset, crimson and gold, hung over the horizon of the clearing: a striking close to a fearful day.

Although the Chinese here had proved so hostile, we were lucky in another way. A few yards inside the curtain of trees we discovered a fine kongsi house, raised well off the ground, approached by a ladder and, what was even better, well supplied with dry lallang grass on top. It was deserted but the roof seemed tolerably intact, and this was lucky too, for rain started to fall again. We undressed completely rather than stay in our soaking garments and I put on a spare shirt, making myself as comfortable as possible on the lallang with my damp groundsheet over me. We may have been fooling ourselves, but we laughed over the incidents of the day and considered ourselves fortunate in having had a good meal before we ran for our lives, and also in spoiling the chances of any pursuit by crossing the swamp. Our only losses were my cap, one I felt keenly, and Elliott's galoshes made from the sheet rubber, but we had covered quite a distance and had a dry lodging for the night.

3rd March. Again what amazing luck! After a reasonable night, undisturbed either by centipedes or scorpions, we gingerly donned our clothes and pushed on through the jungle. To our astonishment we came upon a Chinese refugee settlement within a couple of hundred yards from our starting point, a busy little community of many huts, with women preparing food, children crawling about and general signs of a thriving camp. We were brought to the head of the kongsi who told us that they had come all the way from Mersing. He gave us directions, a plate of rice and a tin of sardines which we ate a little way off to avoid causing any trouble.

Besides getting a good breakfast, we discovered that we had arrived at that long-sought-for oil palm estate, and for a while we toiled on round the perimeter enclosing what must be a huge area. Up till now we had, for the most part, been walking in jungle by day, or at any rate over country which offered us a cover from the sun, but now it beat down unmercifully and we sweated like Trojans in our thick clothing.

Towards the close of the afternoon we came upon a deserted kongsi shack at the edge of the plantation and here we decided to spend the night. We were short of food, so we scrabbled up some remains of tapioca that had been planted in what had obviously been the vegetable garden, and with the roots of that and some keladi (yam) we made a meal that was only bearable because we were hungry. We slept fitfully under some dirty old sacks that we found, but we did have a roof of sorts over our heads which kept out most of the rain which fell later on in the evening.

CHAPTER 8

ON THE RUN –
CENTRAL JOHORE

4th March. Continuing our way round the plantation, towards midday we came on a little clearing at the fringe of the jungle in which was a half-finished dug-out canoe, another trunk on which work had just begun, and up in a tree, some twelve feet off the ground, a little hut approached by a rude ladder. We were looking around when we were startled by a voice saying 'hello', which came from the hut.

To our astonishment the emaciated figure of a man appeared at the door, and we learned that he was a wretched survivor from a number of British soldiers belonging to an artillery unit which had been cut off by the Japanese at Slim River. His was indeed a sad tale. One of a small party of nine which had made its way down to Johore right from the Slim, he had fallen sick (it must have been dysentery). When the party heard of the fall of Singapore, rather than give themselves up they decided to push north again in the hope of eventually getting through to Burma. This fellow, however, had not the strength to keep up with the party and had begged the remainder to go on without him, leaving him in his hideaway with a few provisions.

His companions had told some Chinese at a nearby kongsi of the comrade's plight and they had been looking after him. His mind seemed to be very shaky: his memory was failing, his vitality low and altogether we could not conclude otherwise than that he could not last many more days. We could do nothing for him beyond giving him a tin of bully from our iron rations, and he refused to burden us by accompanying us. He asked us if we thought he ought to give himself up, but since we believed that the Japanese were shooting any stray prisoners who fell into their hands, we did not feel that to do so would be any better than dying in the jungle. After considerable conversation with him and getting his name and regiment for the purpose of recording the meeting, we left, greatly saddened by the experience, the more so as we felt so completely powerless to help or even advise him in any way.

That afternoon we got a meal at a refugee kongsi farther on – the one that was feeding the sick soldier – and there we learned that the Japs had issued an edict ordering all refugees to return to their homes. So it looked as if in the future we would not find it so easy to obtain food and help if all the Chinese left the jungle fringe that we were frequenting.

In the evening we met some more Chinese who were most sympathetic and anxious to help. They gave us a good meal of rice and a little pork, also a tin of milk to take with us. They asked us what news we had, and in return told us about the wretched and oppressive conditions in Johore. We slept in some jungle a mile or so further on, having failed to make much progress by the light of the waning moon, and besides we were getting physically exhausted.

5th March. Early in the morning we got into a rubber estate which, seen from a highish point that had recently been cleared, seemed to stretch for miles. Mosquitoes were terrible, covering one's hands and face, so that we were soon all blotched and swollen. Elliott had to stop to dress a bad blister on a toe and it was agony to stand or sit with the myriads of giant 'tiger' stegamiyas buzzing fiendishly about, all longing to make a meal. I put socks on my hands which helped, but badly missed the cap I had lost.

We came on several deserted shacks and at one I found some unripe papayas and some tapioca root, while Elliott tried to get rice and information from a Chinese who was chopping wood nearby. He returned with a quantity of raw rice and anxious news that the Japs often came round this part looking for provisions and vegetables and that the Chinese was in a state of great alarm. We beat it away from the roadway up a valley, where at the jungle edge we made a fire and cooked rice and papayas. We had a scare when an aeroplane came over, twice, rather lower than we liked and we had to cover everything and get under the shelter of the young rubber trees.

When we were not stifled with smoke the mosquitoes were formidable.

This estate seemed never-ending and it was extremely hilly going, ploughing up and down ravines weighed down with our kit and provisions. We felt we could not go on like this: we were both feeling dead beat, beyond the point where will can overcome exhaustion. So we withdrew into the jungle for a rest and to have a council of war. We went through our kit to see if we could discard anything but decided every item was too valuable. Eventually we decided to drink the tin of milk which we had been given the previous day and finish the remains of the rice flour and toasted rice. Elliott smoked his pipe to keep off the mozzies and we had a good rest until about half past five. We hoped to be able to push on and find some supper before we packed up for the day. Our luck held and after a little while we got an excellent supper from some Chinese who had been employed on the estate. Here, as we had already done so many times, we had to do our best to explain why the British had crumpled up in Malaya and why Singapore, that impregnable fortress, had fallen.

6th March. On this day we reckoned we by-passed Rengam, but it was very trying for we found we had to cross a wide expanse of open country, smallholdings planted with every sort of vegetable and fruit tree, as well as coffee. The Chinese here were very frightened and hostile, would give us no food and repeatedly urged us to enter the jungle. At one point we had a bad scare when we spotted a man who looked just like a Japanese busy at work on a plot with a changkul (hoe). For fully a quarter of an hour we lay low watching the fellow, and it was only when he turned round to reveal his whole face that we knew him for a Chinese.

Once back in the jungle we found a network of paths, all obviously well used. This fact and our discovery of many deserted shacks and shelters in the jungle fringe made us conclude that this had been a popular area for refugees from the battle zone near Kluang which lay perhaps 15-20 miles to our north and was our next objective. On our way we met with several parties of Chinese laden with household goods, rice, etc., who told us they were returning to

54

their homes as a result of a Japanese decree.

All that afternoon we toiled along a well-defined jungle rentis (a cut made by Forest Rangers), often climbing steeply, eventually coming out in a rubber estate: here we found a deserted refugee shack where we stopped for the night. It was a lovely evening and I remember how pleasant it was to be sitting in the sunset light, with a little stream chuckling away at our feet, while I waited for the water to boil in the billy.

The next day, 7th March, we made very little progress: we got into the jungle intersected by paths, none of which seemed to help us much, and we wasted a lot of time examining deserted refuges. At one of them we found two kittens and a young dog, very frightened; we cooked ourselves a meal, trying some pickled radish which we found with our rice (it was not nice). We gave some rice to the dog which ate greedily.

As we were about to leave, two young Chinese lads came up to collect the odds and ends. We were glad the animals were to be taken and offered to return the pickles and a bottle of iodine which we had also scrounged. The Chinese however did not seem concerned about these two items and said we could keep them. We were glad for the iodine as it was strong stuff and would help Elliott's Singapore foot.

In the evening we came out at a point where the thin jungle bordered the railway line and also the road. Elliott squinted out and saw quite a lot of traffic on the road and some Japanese military cars. Trains came down the line too and we wondered whether we might be able to use the line at night. There was a Chinese hut across the road, so after dark we crept across in search of food. We found three Chinese in the hut who would not give us a meal, but gave us a quantity of raw rice, saying we could get a meal at the kongsi house up the road. So we made our way along the edge of the road, falling in and out of rubber silt-trenches.

Suddenly we saw car lights coming down the road, and in my haste to get up a bank from the verge into the rubber I lost the parang which was secured round my waist and we spent an anxious twenty minutes searching for the precious weapon in the dark. We eventually found the kongsi and after much knocking and calling roused the occupants, two Chinese, who appeared to be the caretakers of the place. They agreed to give us a meal if we would wait in the rubber, and in half an hour they brought along big bowls of rice and some meat: it was only tulang babi, pig bones, they said apologetically, but it was all they had and you may imagine none the less welcome to us. We tucked into this greedily, enjoying the scraps of meat and the delicious flavour of the bones, chatting to one of the Chinese the while. He dilated on the hard times, how the Japanese were always stopping at their place for a meal, how scarce things were and how expensive and difficult it was to get rice. We left with profuse thanks and retraced our steps to the jungle to sleep.

8th March. We again made very little progress in this disconcerting district: paths we tried to follow kept on petering out and finally after hours of useless trudging we hacked our way back to the railway through dense jungle growth. For some days now we had not been satisfied with the progress we were making. We had been over three weeks on our trek and were still in central Johore south of Kluang and although we might have covered 150 miles or so on foot, we had barely gone half that distance as the crow flies. Our boots were wearing out, our strength declining. However could we possibly reach our goal at this rate? We decided to try another way: the railway. We realised that it might be risky – we had no idea of what the Japanese would have in the way of patrols, blocks, guards, etc. – but we reckoned it might be worth it. We were sick of plodding and cutting our way through difficult country.

We waited for night to fall – how devilish the mosquitoes were in that rubber on the other side of the line – and then, since nothing happened in the way of enemy activity, boldly struck out for Kluang.

The going was good and we felt we were justified in trying this experiment. It is true we had one or two frights: once when a fast light engine came dashing round a corner and we had to hurl ourselves into the long grass at the side; and again when we were in a cutting and had to run like hell to get out before an oncoming train caught us in the glare of its headlights. They were goods trains, but we saw Japanese soldiers in the engine cabs. On and on we walked like automata, our bodies loads of weariness, the midnight hours passing with leaden minutes. We passed Menkipol station: no guard, no sign of any sentry. One o'clock, two o'clock: we still walked on.

The last quarter of the moon came up and cast a wan light over the landscape. To our right we could see the dark outline of a mountain ridge, and then ahead we saw a light. We did not bother much about this as it appeared to be off the railway line, and then we came to a gate on which was a notice in English, Malay and Chinese: 'No Thoroughfare'. The Malay version read 'Ta buleh jalang sini': it was quite easy to read in the moonlight. Elliott studied this and the gateway with old Daneite wiring on either side, and I remarked that I supposed it was an old block left by the Australians — it was just how they might spell 'jalan' with a 'g' — and we walked straight into the trap! A few yards further along the embankment we were abruptly challenged in Japanese. What fools we had been! Our brains had been so numbed by exhaustion and fatigue that we failed to scout round this obstruction. Our first thought was to get out of this pickle and we plunged down the embankment, only to find ourselves facing more Daneite fencing. Our only way out was the way we had come in, I hissed to Elliott. So up the embankment we scrambled, dashed along the twenty yards or so to the gate, every moment expecting to be shot in the backside, and then broke away down the embankment in the direction of the mountain we had noticed before.

In a few minutes we stopped to take breath and make a plan. Elliott had lost his groundsheet in the flight, a pity for it would certainly be found and it would be known that we were soldiers. Possibly the Japs might take us for a party trying to do a demolition on the line — and then what? Hunt us down? Use bloodhounds perhaps? Taken altogether the prospects did not seem too rosy if we stayed on the spot. We decided to make tracks for that sizeable mountain which lay to the east.

We found a small stream so we splashed into this and waded up it for a quarter-mile, just in case the Japs tried to track with hounds, and then we found we had got into a patch of very thick belukar.

Further progress was impossible in the dark so, wet up to our middles as we were, we curled up in the thick undergrowth and dozed, anxiously waiting for the dawn to break.

At the very first sign of light I roused Elliott and off we set: fortunately the belukar shortly gave way to rubber and we simply galloped over the ground which rose steadily in the lower slopes of the mountain. We came across some Chinese squatters' huts and I asked at one place if they could give us anything. They seemed scared to see us – no wonder – and refused, but relented so far as to allow me a drink of water from the well and referred us to another house. Here they were equally frightened but gave us some sweet potatoes and mouldy cakes made from rice flour.

To our relief we reached the jungle fringe without any apparent noises of a search in our rear and we stopped for a rest and to eat the rice cakes. We thought however that we had better be on the safe side and put a few more miles between us and those confounded Japs; accordingly we pushed into the forest reserve and found a track which led us conveniently and gently up the mountain in a northerly direction and away from the centre of disturbance. At one point we descended a little to where a track led up to a quarry; just below was a Chinese kongsi which I approached for food and news. They were jumpy there and obviously embarrassed by my presence, but gave me some sweet rice cracknel cakes and some other leathery cakes to go on with. I moved off quickly when told that another Chinese had reported Japanese searching in parties in this direction.

Not long after we had moved off again we heard the sound of shots being fired singly and in bursts as from a tommy-gun and this, as you may guess, helped to lend wings to our feet. We gradually climbed up and up, passed what we thought were the headworks of Kluang's water supply, always finding a convenient path. From time to time we got glimpses of Kluang far away and beneath us, and always the noise of shooting continued, now intensified and now dying away. Having got so far up the mountain we agreed that we might as well go to the very top and lie low there where no one would dream of coming until the hue and cry should die down, and there too we might get a good view of the country round and see what might be our best route.

The ascent was heartbreaking. We were both extremely tired and not in the best condition to do a stiff climb. However after a couple of hours and many rests, to our great joy we came out of the thin jungle into an area of sparse bracken that covers the tops of most mountains in Malaya. In a few moments we were at the top, a rounded little plateau with a trig. post at the summit.

The sun was out, a pleasant breeze blew, we took off our clothes and boots and dried everything on the ground or hanging on bushes. We even munched a few raisins and ate a few grains of sugar by way of picnicking at such a delightful spot. The shooting still went on and we laughed at getting out of our scrape. We had a good look at the view spread beneath us, the greater part of Kluang to the north-west, including the airfield on which glittered the silvery form of a big two-engined bomber. To the north we could see successive layers of rubber, kampong land, jungle, what might be oil palms and, beyond that, yet more jungle which stretched in an undulating vista to the horizon. We also thought we would trace the outline of the Kluang-Mersing road which we would have to cross some time.

The shooting continued well into the afternoon. Besides that the only jarring note to disturb our harmony was an aeroplane which flew right over the summit where we were and to our dismay returned five minutes later. On the first occasion we had not been quite quick enough to remove all our clothing from sight, but the second time round you may be sure we left nothing tell-tale visible.

The evening we spent on the slopes of Kluang Hill remains one of the happiest memories of the trip: it was an idyllic moment among the excitements and hardships we encountered each day. It was a time of great peace of mind and body after the helter-skelter of the previous twenty-four hours. We left the summit at about 4.30 with the idea of camping where we first found water and we cannot have descended more than a few hundred feet in a surprisingly semi-perpendicular manner (we did not follow the way we came) before we came upon a secluded ravine with plenty of jungle cover in which a tiny stream issued from a spring in the rocky face. This was just perfect for us. As dusk fell we lit a fire – using dry sticks and bracken collected from the summit to avoid making much smoke — and before long had a good meal of rice and sweet potatoes. I usually ate my portion off a leaf while Elliott used the billy-lid. We were indeed happy perched high in our mountain eyrie, and again congratulated ourselves on our good fortune while Elliott smoked a pipe and I boiled water for our bottles, enjoying the fresh atmosphere of our lofty camp. It was a joy to be entirely free from mosquitoes in the cool and energising air of an altitude of 1,000 feet above sea level.

CHAPTER 9

AMONG THE JAKUN

10th March. We had been free for three weeks and in that time we had traversed half the State of Johore and had had a run of amazing luck. Apart from sheer exhaustion we had kept in good condition and mercifully had not contracted any tropical disease which so speedily drags a man down to weakness and death. The latter part of this adventure will reveal how helpless a person is once malaria secures a hold, and how such an attempt as ours was doomed to failure since we had no drugs to fight it.

We slept late, rose and cooked breakfast in a leisurely manner, as we intended to lie up here in the mountain all the forenoon and for once in a while were in no hurry to get on. Afterwards, when I had just been easing myself a little way downstream, I got one of the shocks of my life to see a huge dog, as big as an Alsatian but not of that breed, only a few yards away at the edge of a small ravine. The dog heard me and started back as if he had been every bit as surprised as me, and made off through the jungle yelping in a startled manner until he was lost to our hearing. What on earth was the meaning of this, that such a devil-hound should break in upon our peaceful solitude? Eventually Elliott and I discounted the idea that it could be in any way connected with the Japanese search and I concluded that it was probably a dog which had been forced to go wild in the jungle after being abandoned by its peace-time owners. We did however make ready to move at a moment's notice, and then lay down to doze and sleep the hours away without paying any attention to the noise of firearms which continued to pop off at intervals in a desultory way, as if the keenness of yesterday's chase had dwindled away. We were surprised at the Japanese wasting such a lot of ammunition over us and we thought that they were probably beating large thickets, firing and shouting at the same time to scare us and make us give ourselves away.

61

Soon after three o'clock we moved off, going slowly as the undergrowth was thick and prickly, but after about an hour we came out into the rubber where an estate reached high up the hillside. We did not want to come down too soon before dusk, so we rested and enjoyed the view. That bomber was still there. We really were in a horribly nervous condition, always straining to catch any sound, always glancing sharply about in case anyone should spot us, and I supposed this was not surprising as we had been living on very little besides nervous energy. Two scanty meals a day, and rice at that, is not the best sort of diet for our precarious existence. But then this was my first experience of being the hunted and having to preserve life by quickness of wit and action.

A little later we had another scare when we were skirting some coolie lines in the same estate. A Tamil behind some outbuildings spotted us and after a good look in our direction ran back to the lines. 'Oh, hell!' we thought, 'that's torn it! A Tamil too! He is bound to have heard of the search and will give us away.' We scampered off post-haste, jumping ditches and scrambling up banks, with the object of reaching the Mersing road before news of our whereabouts could be conveyed to the Japanese. Suddenly, to our great surprise, we caught sight of the road some fifty yards away through the rubber. We had not expected to come to it so soon. We slumped on our bellies in a rubber trench to watch it. There was far too much traffic about for us to cross it just then: cars, bullock carts, cyclists of every race, Japs in military cars. A Tamil came up the road to the estate with a sack of rice on his bicycle, but no one went down it from the coolie lines. We began to breathe more easily: perhaps the Tamil who had spotted us took us for Jap soldiers after all.

Towards dusk the traffic on the road dwindled and we slipped across without any fuss into the rubber on the other side. We kept on a compass bearing and an hour or so later landed up at a Chinese squatter's house where we got the most friendly welcome. 'Tuan, Tuan,' the old lady repeated in joyful surprise when she realised I was a European: it was most touching! We fed well on rice and pork and long beans and then slept until the moon, now in its last quarter, rose to give us enough light to travel.

11th March. We had resolved to get out of this dangerous locality with all possible speed and that was why we pushed on in the early hours of the morning. If we could manage it we wanted to reach the belt of jungle that we had noticed from the top of the mountain. We had found out the names of two villages further up the line, Nyior and Chembi, and we intended to cut across the jungle and meet the railway line at either of those two places and then follow it up as we had done before. With this idea, therefore, we took a bearing on a star in the direction of which a friendly Chinese had assured us Nyior lay, and pursued our way across open country past Malay kampongs and Chinese squatter houses, always using paths where they served our purpose. We took with us a bundle of rice with some salt soya beans which the Chinese pressed upon us.

We kept on without a break for well over three hours until, as dawn was breaking, we reached the jungle belt. Far to our left we could see the grand outline of Kluang Mountain and Elliott took a back-bearing on it which was all right. It is curious how certain moments are impressed upon my memory: these were occasions when time seemed to stop and when it needed a tremendous effort to drag oneself back to the cold light of reality, to remember that we were runaways, aliens in a strange land, for whom it was dangerous to think too much about the future or the beauties of nature which lay around us. It was one such moment when I stood on the hill by the jungle's edge, looked towards Kluang and saw the sun rise in a perfect blaze of glory over the mountain.

We now had no other course but to cross this strip of jungle and to our chagrin it turned out to be swamp. We tried to follow a bearing but it was a heartbreaking job. The nipah thorns were absolutely relentless, tearing at our skin, our clothes. They have a nasty habit of breaking off when they stick into you, which aggravates matters. In addition to the nipah there was plenty of mengkuang, a plant of the pineapple family, of which the prickly leaves are used in weaving and mat-making. The day was drawing in and we were wondering how long this would continue. I myself scarcely dared hope we would get out of it that night: I just ploughed on like an automaton. Then once again luck was with us: the cover of the trees began to thin, the ground became perceptibly drier and firmer and just as it was growing dusk we were overjoyed to get out of the morass and find ourselves in a little newly-planted banana patch. It was then that our bundle of rice and beans came in so very handy.

Still we pressed on through rubber, then through a much neglected oil palm estate for maybe a couple of hours in the gathering darkness under the twinkling stars. We were looking for some sign of habitation, for food and directions as usual. At last we spied a light in the distance and soon the sound of that lovely tune which has become the national anthem of Malaysia — Terang Bulan — came to our ears. We hastened towards it: surely we would find friends there. It was a kongsi house all right, but they had no food to spare; however they gave us bowls of the most delicious sweet coffee and a guide to set us on the road to another kongsi where we would be sure to get a meal. It was on the way to Chembi too, they said. A young Chinese accompanied us for a mile or so, taking us by side paths through the oil palms, and then left us where a goodish track led towards the other kongsi and the jungle proper. The way was long but we trudged on and on, passing one house deserted but for three Chinese. This was not the right one and so we went on again. The Great Bear rose ahead of us.

At long last our patience was rewarded and we received a splendid welcome on our arrival. Moreover we had the best meal since the beginning of our escapade, for this was the last night of the many refugees at this kongsi before they returned to their homes in Kluang and they had killed a pig. Besides rice and pork there was tofu (bean curd) and beans and several sorts of vegetables. Of course we had to give all the news we could and we spent a good hour talking with them and gleaning every scrap that might help us. It must have been midnight when we left to pick a place a little farther on and sleep soundly until dawn.

12th March. All morning we followed a path which we had been told would bring us to a kampong where many Chinese had fled for refuge. This was on the further side of a biggish river which, since

64

it flowed west to Kluang, we would have to cross. Our journey was uneventful until we reached the river, except we smelled tiger at one point. Elliott said we must have passed within twenty or thirty feet of it.

Peering through the undergrowth at the river bank we got another shock when we saw what appeared to be a Japanese soldier sitting in the bow of a small dugout canoe which was being paddled by a Malay at the stern. This was a terrible thing, to find Japs right in the ulu after having done our best to steer clear of them. Perhaps it was a Jap overseeing the compulsory return of refugees? At any rate we lay low and watched the river for a couple of hours. Several punts and canoes loaded with Chinese went downstream; one or two Malays busy with fishing passed to and fro. Not a sign of any Japanese. Then a strange-looking Malay, paddling an old dugout, came upstream and started fishing in a little creek within a few yards of us. I decided he must be a Jakun and told Elliott that the man we mistook for a Japanese must have been one of these Jakun wearing an odd bit of an old felt hat. So I called politely to this fisherman and asked if he would ferry the two of us across the river, about twenty yards or so at this point. With a nod and a 'Baik, Tuan', and without a moment's hesitation, he put by his rod and paddled over to me. It was a tricky journey, one at a time, with barely half an inch of freeboard, but he took us across safely and pointed in the direction of the kampong.

When we came upon it at last we found it was a Malay settlement. It was our first contact with Malays and we felt distinctly nervous after all the bad reports we had heard about them. However I approached one house and talked with an oldish man. I asked for Chembi or Nyior and he pointed in their direction. Then he mentioned that there was a Jakun kampong not far off, and since they were acquainted with the jungle they might help us more than he could. I also had a few words with a young Malay who had been in the Government Survey Department and had run away to safety. There was little point in staying longer so we said, 'Selamat tinggal' and made our way with some difficulty to the little Jakun settlement, a group of some five or six houses which we soon learned was called

Pekan Bantal. This was my first experience of a Jakun kampong and I was immensely interested.

The houses were Malay in style but of a poor type, just woven bamboo walls and atap with a few banana and other fruit trees growing round about. They were not nearly so clean and tidy as the ones I had been used to in Malacca. For one thing there was little furniture. One or two fish traps lay around. Behind, land had been cleared where tapioca was growing; I also noticed maize and some sweet potato plants. We met the headman of this little kampong; he looked half Malay and half Jakun, but spoke excellent Malay. He professed Islam, and from one thing and another I gathered that although he called himself 'Orang Hutan' and 'Sakai' he was really more Malay than anything else.

Our meeting with him considerably changed our plans of making our way upcountry. He was very sympathetic and told us that some ten days before he had helped two other Europeans and some Indian soldiers in similar circumstances. In addition he told us of the existence of a number of jungle kampongs spaced out in a string through Johore up to Ulu Segamat and suggested we might make our way north by proceeding from one kampong to another. It came on to rain so we sheltered beneath his house and talked at length of how to reach these other villages. He even drew us little plans and diagrams. We decided to try this scheme and so be quit of the Japs if we could.

The day was closing in. The rain still kept on falling gently, so I plucked up courage to ask if he could give us some shelter for the night and cook us some food. He agreed. We gave him half a billy of rice and some sweet potatoes and in half an hour he brought down from the kitchen two plates of rice, two hardboiled eggs, a plate of cooked tapioca root, a tapioca chapati and, best of all, a fish, beautifully baked on hot embers. We even had a scraping of margarine to put on the chapati and a little salt. After this excellent and satisfying meal Ahmad, for such was his name, led us to a little hut that was unoccupied and left us in peace for the night.

Friday 13th March. Soon after daylight we went down to Ahmad's. He was up and he said his wife was just cooking the chapatis. We also saw the little Jakun who had ferried us across the river, Ahmad's brother apparently. There were three or four women visible and a few children, but on the whole it was not a very lively place. Ahmad again gave us minute directions and set off with us for half a mile. But alas! the directions were far from clear. Once in the jungle the track had many forks: which to take? After a couple of hours we came out into a big clearing, the work of Chinese squatters who proved to be Hokkien and not at all friendly.

While we were eating some cold rice and dried fish, Elliott said they were discussing whether they should detain us and call the Japanese. You may imagine we did not like them at all and cleared out quickly. Then we lost our way: rain came on and we got thoroughly miserable and depressed. How could we ever find the jungle rentis that Ahmad said would take us straight to Paloh? After wandering ineffectually for several hours we got fed up and managed to retrace our steps quickly to Pekan Bantal, which we reached with our tails between our legs at about dusk. Ahmad was very sick to see us again as he was nervous about harbouring us and afraid of blabbing tongues. He packed us off to the little hut and we did not have nearly such a good supper that night.

14th March. To make quite sure we found the rentis all right this time, Ahmad, accompanied by another brother, a fine-looking Malay, guided us by jungle paths right to the head of the rentis. They walked at a terrific pace and we were hard put to keep up. Ahmad from time to time would tell us interesting facts about the jungle, how to find fruits and catch game. A Jakun, he said, an 'Orang Hutan' such as he was, could live in the jungle for a month on end by his wits and not starve. We thanked him profusely, said we hoped we would meet again and set off down the rentis. Originally some six feet wide it marked the boundary of a jungle reserve and every 220 yards we could expect to find the Forest Department plate nailed to a tree: 'Hutan Simpan'. The number of the plate where Ahmad left us was 564; we would have to pass forty of these to cover five miles, he said, before we would come out of the jungle.

From what Ahmad said, that rentis had been newly cleared in July or August of the preceding year, but if that was so this was an example of how quickly and relentlessly the Malay jungle leaps up after the hand of man has cleared it. For a few score yards maybe the rentis would be fairly free, then we would be faced by all the horrors of the jungle: fallen trees, creepers, nipah, mengkuang and swamp.

Through thick and thin we ploughed, Elliott generally leading the way. Without him, I confess, I would have missed the way time after time, but somehow he seemed to have a knack of hitting on the trail. By means of compass and perhaps a little sixth sense and a lot of luck, we never lost the rentis for long and now and again we would see a plate nailed up and the serial number would be diminishing. We rested several times but never stopped to eat and altogether, from the time we parted from our guide, we must have been on the go for six or seven hours when dusk began to creep on. In that time, judging by the Forest Department number plates, we had only covered four and a half miles. We were quite fagged out, so we decided to stop where we were, have a meal and trust that it would not rain on us. It didn't.

Sunday 15th March. A further hour's trek brought us out of the jungle, thank heaven, and we found the big Pinang (betel nut palm) estate to which Ahmad had directed us. So far so good. Now we had to find the entrance to the jungle path which would bring us to the second Jakun village of Tamoh. Eventually we got in touch with the clerk of the estate who gave us a good meal of bubor, sardines and biscuits but who was pretty scornful of us and not of much real help.

We might have spent the rest of the day vainly searching for the track had we not landed up at the house of a charming Hailam, who we gathered had been a foreman on the estate for years and who had now retired. He and his wife and family all turned out when we arrived. They sat us down, brought us coffee and biscuits and we had a great time. The son, aged twenty, was particularly helpful, brought Elliott a mackintosh cape in place of the one he had lost at Kluang and said there was an old Chinese who knew all the jungle paths and that he would surely set us on the right one for Tamoh. Off we went, with the good wishes of all and some provisions as well, found the Chinese and were put speedily on our way. This seemed a propitious send-off and we set off in high hopes: only to find after half a mile we were faced with a perplexing fork, as usual. We took the left hand one and soon after camped for the night at a spot where an old shack had once been.

16th March. This day we were frustrated and disappointed and failed to get anywhere. We found we had got into a tangled maze of paths in a jelutong tapping area, so in despair we retraced our steps right back past our recent campsite to the very first fork and tried the right hand path. After practically wasting the whole day, what made us even more annoyed was that when we camped that evening we just missed catching a fine iguana!

17th March. To our great relief our wanderings were shortened by our stumbling upon the hut of a jungle dweller, a Chinese who made a living by tapping jelutong trees and collecting the latex which, being used as the base for chewing gum, had formerly commanded a high value. This man eked out a tolerable existence in these hard days by growing vegetables in the plot around his house: this latter was a humble affair, only a single room, built of rough-hewn timber and bamboo, thatched with leaves of jungle plants.

His wife and son had quarters of their own: a tiny shelter built in a tree some twenty feet from the ground and approached by a rude ladder. This was a precaution against wild beasts. The old man was out when we turned up early in the forenoon, but with typical Chinese hospitality the wife pressed food on us. She was a 'nonya', a Straits-born woman from Singapore, and had lived in Malacca for many years so was able to speak Malay well.

We thought it best to wait for the husband to return from Paloh and we whiled away the hours chatting with the old lady who smoked a silver Chinese hubble-bubble and fussed over the brat who appeared to be suffering from adenoids. I walked outside, had a wash in the clear little stream, and watched the lovely jungle butterflies as they executed their dance where the little boy had relieved himself: a novel way to me of attracting lepidoptera! In the bed of the stream were lying scores of blocks of jelutong, in cold storage until better times should reopen the market for this valuable product.

Towards evening the husband returned; his wife quickly explained the situation and he agreed to guide us to the house of another jelutong tapper not far away who would give us hospitality for the night and would know how to reach Tamoh. The man hurriedly swallowed a bowl of bubor and led us off, setting a pace that took us helter-skelter up hill and down ravines by the most tortuous paths through the jungle, so that in a few minutes we were absolutely gasping for breath and sweating from every pore. An hour of this breakneck progress brought us to the edge of the clearing where our guide left us; he would not stop to introduce such a couple of runaways.

The solitary Chinese whom we found at home busy finishing his supper was a queer character. At first he was very difficult and pretended not to understand a word of Malay, but acquaintance soon loosened his tongue a little. He told us that times were hard and that jelutong tapping did not pay now, so he had turned over to the manufacture of wooden tubs, many of which in various stages of completion were visible from the hut. In addition we gathered his time was not entirely taken up by such employment, for after supper, with a sly look, he brought out a bottle of excellent samsu (rice brandy) and with a cunning smile and a gesture he intimated that he was able to bamboozle a harmless government by keeping his illegal still well hidden in the depths of the jungle. As an ex-magistrate accustomed to dealing with such illegal distilleries, I was highly tickled.

Altogether we spent a most amusing evening with this fellow, whom we nicknamed Inscrutable Manchu from his unusual appearance and cast of countenance. We were all the more intrigued by him because his manner indicated the European house-trained 'boy' rather than the unsophisticated coolie. What was more his cooking was superb! As we sat outside in the cool evening air, Elliott smoking his pipe while I watched the stars come out over the clearing, I wondered at our good fortune and hoped he would be as good a guide on the morrow.

18th March. Before it was properly light our host was up, busy cooking rice and frying pumpkin. With this and a tin of sardines thrown in, we made an excellent breakfast and set off immediately for Tamoh. Our Chinese friend put us on the right path and after some three or four hours we came across the first signs of Jakun. At one point where the path ran along the bank of a stream we noticed a palisade of stakes placed so as to deflect the current to one side. On looking closer we saw two fish traps set in the opening that remained: beautiful pieces of work fashioned from thin bamboo twigs, shaped like a funnel at the open end and tapering to a point at the rear. Later we noticed several more traps and at one point when we were casting round for further signs of Jakun I happened to notice a hut or shelter built some thirty feet up in a tree, and concluded that this was one of the Jakun hunting boxes, although perhaps more typical of Sakai. No one was at home, and on examining it closer the hut proved to be dilapidated.

We continued upstream and about half an hour later heard the sound of someone chopping wood not so very far off. This raised our hopes and we hurried off through the jungle undergrowth in the direction of the sound. There we found a Jakun and his young son, a well-built lad of about twelve, busy felling a tree. They did not seem particularly surprised at our approach, and in answer to my enquiries whether he could show us the way to Tamoh he replied that it was only a mile further upstream and that he himself would take us to the headman's house.

Soon we came to houses scattered here and there indiscriminately among the acres of towering tapioca. They seemed to be humble dwellings of Malay style and similar to the ones at Pekan Bantal. Women sat listlessly at the doors, fowls and goats scratched about underneath, but children did not seem much in evidence. The headman's house was rather more substantial than the others. He himself was out but his brother invited us in and we sat in the deep verandah and talked. On the walls hung a pair of fine hunting spears with terrible-looking barbs; there were some fishing spears too, of smaller size. Besides these the only other ornaments were a brass drum and a 'tambour' or small hand drum which I examined eagerly. Furniture there was none. We asked if they could boil us some water and after some delay they brought us a brass cooking pot with some awful-tasting tepid water in it. I asked where it came from. 'The river,' they said in some surprise. 'Have you no wells?' I asked. 'Oh, no,' was the reply, 'the river is quite good enough'!

Tapioca was the staple article of their diet and besides they got fish from the river: they did not grow rice. Among other things we learned that they were very worried about a serious disease which was affecting members of their women-folk. They had tried to get medicine from the shops at Bekoh and Paloh, but it had been of no use. The worldly-wise Elliott suggested that they might be suffering from syphilis. Certainly as we passed through it the place did not seem to be at all thriving: the dirt round some of the huts was appalling. I tried to persuade one of the Jakun to guide us to the next village, but they were a canny crowd and were obviously looking for a promise of hard cash beforehand. But we disappointed them as we had nothing to give away and so we left after being shown the right path.

Our route followed the twisting course of the river as it wound through the ever-deepening ravines to its watershed. It was most picturesque – what pleasure, we reflected, it would have afforded us if we were on a holiday trip – but we were getting exhausted and had little time for the beauties of nature. We gathered and ate a number of little fruits which were bitter-sweet and gave us a sore mouth: they had a yellow skin and were the size of a plum, quite refreshing really. Towards evening we camped at a lovely spot where the stream came tumbling down over rocks. We had been climbing steadily and must have been several hundred feet above sea level as the atmosphere was delightfully cool. Moreover since we had entered the jungle at Paloh we had not been bothered by mosquitoes. Leeches there were in plenty, especially after rain, but we had got quite used to them now and our lower clothing was almost proof against them if we could stop and pick them off from time to time.

CHAPTER 10

OVERTAKEN BY FEVER

19th March. Today we went over that watershed. The stream which we left would eventually flow out into the Straits of Malacca, while the one down to which we now came would, we believed, reach the East Coast at Endau. Our next Jakun village was named Kemedak, and this we reached after a hard morning, tramping through rain and up the actual bed of the river.

Elliott was not feeling very well and it was when he was having a rest that I pushed on ahead and found the kampong. We approached the place with some diffidence after the rather cool reception we had got at the last village, but when we went up to a hut with sides open all round in which some half dozen men were sitting, we were received fairly well. An old chap asked if we had eaten and, when we said no, cooked us a dish of the most delicious rice I have ever tasted. It was freshly pounded from the hill padi grown in that locality and it had a quality similar to that of coarsely ground oatmeal, a rare aroma that was most pleasing. To go with this we had an 'ulam' or relish made from banana shoots and chillies, hot and piquant. Salt however was short, and we were given a few crystals to go with our rice, there being none in the banana ulam. This primitive shelter was stacked with sacks of padi in the centre, and on the further side the women sat, segregated from the males. The men busied themselves on odd jobs, one plaiting a carrying basket, another whittling away at a piece of wood with a parang.

Conversation was general, about the shortage of salt and tobacco and so on. These people, well out of touch with civilisation, hardly knew what it meant that the country had passed under an alien rule.

I made discreet enquiries as to whether they could guide us to the next village, named Juaseh, and whether they could provide us with some shelter for the night. They hedged a bit and were obviously waiting for an offer of money, so I had to admit in the end that we had not got any, and then they seemed disappointed. However they eventually led us past clearings of tapioca and hill padi and across the river to an empty hut where we could lodge. Elliott lay down with a raging headache and I was pestered all the afternoon by some inquisitive youngsters. In trying to get hold of a guide I used every sort of persuasion and at last one fellow said he would see us 'over the mountain'. They gave us a little raw rice, some tapioca and a couple of hens' eggs: a lad brought a gourdful of water and I cooked on the 'dapor' (hearth) in our hut. Elliott was feeling too bad to eat much and we were both glad to get to bed when darkness put an end to the visits of these inquisitive folk.

20th March. Although Elliott was pretty sick we resolved to push off as soon we could rather than stay among people who were not friendly towards us. I cooked more tapioca root for breakfast and also boiled four eggs which I shamelessly took from the fowls' nest under the house. Two Jakun came with us, one a new face, a fellow who knew the way, the other the old man who had cooked the rice the previous day. He carried a blowpipe and a little quiver of darts and said they wanted to shoot some monkeys. The guide carried a woven basket filled with freshly dug tapioca roots; a parang completed his gear.

Our way led up the river Kemedak towards the mountains that separated us from Segamat District, and it was by no means a picnic. Now we waded knee-deep up the river bed, sometimes on slippery stones, now on the heights above the river, striking straight up the towering hills. Evidently the Jakun were trying to follow the trail of some Malays who had gone that way some days before, and I must say their tracking was wonderful: their eyes unerringly picked up the tiniest clues. But trying to keep up with them nearly killed us. The old man with the blowpipe jumped ahead like a stag, and we were horribly outdone. We cursed them for leading us on this goose chase, but all to no purpose, for eventually we came down to the river again, and so wasted all that energy for nothing. Soon we arrived at a point where the river forked and here the Jakun said goodbye after giving us instructions as to how to proceed. We were now both so exhausted that we camped at the first suitable spot, a place where we found an old Jakun shelter waiting for us. I tried to wash some of my clothes but Elliott felt feverish and did nothing. Then I developed a headache too, and we wondered what on earth was the matter with us.

21st March. Elliott now felt too ill to move and we agreed to stop where we were. I also felt feverish during the day.

22nd March. Our plight was miserable, but we had to make a start – we had enough rice for three more meals only – so we toiled and toiled along the river bed, up a tributary that petered out, and then struck off to the left along a steep path which led over the watershed.

I should mention that the views of jungle-covered mountain tops beetling around us were sometimes grand, and as we came over the pass we had a long vista down a side valley, always jungle of course, with a tree here and there in bloom or change of leaf showing up in that expanse of apparent sameness. Once over the top we felt we could rest. My fever came on badly and Elliott left me while he got a fire going to boil some rice. In a little while I felt better and rejoined him. We sacrificed a tin of baked beans, part of our iron rations, to see if that would put any fresh strength into us. I remember very little of the rest of that day, struggling down the upper reaches of the Juaseh river.

We camped that night using an old Jakun shelter: my fever left me temporarily.

23rd March. Downstream again we toiled, now in the river, now cutting our way through the jungle, or trying to find a decent path which the Jakun assured us we would strike. My fever came on again at noon preceded by a violent bout of shivering. Yes, this must be the malaria we had been so much dreading: nothing else could recur with such regularity. Elliott had fever too, though his did not keep the same timetable as mine. Then after my temperature had risen and risen I would break out into a gentle sweat and would thank God that the fever had gone for the time being. Then I would perk up, talk with Elliott, be able to appreciate something of the grand scenery, and the rest of the evening followed by sweet sleep would be a blessed release after the hellish slog of the day. No quinine, no quinine! What fools we had been to venture on such an undertaking without any supplies of this drug! Well, we would just have to get some or pass out, unknown and uncared for in the depths of the merciless jungle.

That evening our tempers were short: it was the first time in over four weeks that we had lost patience with each other, but even that did not last long, and we set to and built ourselves a shelter of palm leaves on a sandbank by the river's edge and had a meal. Above the massive jungle trees the delicate slip of the new moon rose and hung like some magic symbol over the cleft which the river made in the otherwise unbroken canopy of green. The stars came out one by one. We slept.

24th March. Our third day downstream. Slog, slog, squelch and splash, hacking our way one moment, slipping down slopes the next. Fever again at midday. Walking like an automaton down the river bed all the long length of the afternoon. Then at last we met Jakun: this was Ulu Juaseh. Juaseh proper was further on and one man offered to show the way. On and on, however could I endure? But still on and on. Past squalid huts ... Ulu Juaseh I supposed, and how I would have liked to stop there! But no, on still further to Juaseh. When our guide left us he told us to go straight on, through a new clearing, and the village would be about a mile distant. But we lost the path through the clearing and had a terrible time climbing over felled half-burnt trees. We must have done that mile five times over. Those low-down, lying Jakun! Then at nightfall, quite worn out, we came, to our surprise, upon a Chinese kongsi — woodcutters without a doubt — and here we had the most gloomy and unprepossessing welcome of any on our trip. The people there just ignored us, and it took all my arts of persuasion to make them take pity on our plight and give us a meal. The towkay gave us some directions and advised us not to go to Tenang as the loyalty of the Malays there was doubtful: he said we should turn off to the right and make for another Jakun village called Segamat Kechik which lay right in the depths of the jungle.

25th March. The directions, as so often, turned out to be hopeless and we lost our way completely. At midday I was overcome by my fever, so we lay low until the evening by which time I had slept it off. There was still one more way to try, now that it was dark, other than taking the road to Tenang, so we struck out once again soon landing up at little Chinese shack, a refugee shelter where we found two young Chinese. These welcomed us heartily, gave us a meal, told us all their news and said they would help us on the way to Segamat. One of the lads was a goldsmith who had kept a shop in Tenang. He had given that up now and was cultivating vegetables out here instead. The other had recently been up to Kuala Lumpur, by train. He described how the Japanese allowed the local people to ride on the roofs of the carriages and trucks while the troops sat inside. Travel appeared to be free at this stage of the occupation, but at each person's own risk, of course. On the trip that this fellow had made, one Chinese had fallen off the roof of the train while asleep and been killed. We were also given some grisly reports of conditions in the capital. There had been a round-up of Chinese guerillas not far from the town: every one of them, women and children as well, had been massacred and the heads of some who had been decapitated had been stuck on poles and exhibited in public places. A white girl, too, they said, had been exposed naked to the public gaze outside the Robinson building. I must say we thought this a bit far-fetched and discounted the story, but at this time we did not know to what extremes Japanese barbarity could go.

We set off well after midnight, feeling much refreshed, with the two lads showing us the way by striking matches frequently: after expending scores of them they landed us safely on the bund of a new irrigation area which we now had to follow. The way was plain and for several hours we walked along the bund, past vast fields of padi and many Malay houses, all quiet at this time of the night. Finally we came to the headworks of the irrigation scheme, incomplete so far as we could judge, and by means of the sluice bridge crossed the river which appeared to be about 80 feet wide at this spot. Just beyond we lay down to sleep until daylight.

It was now pretty clear we were in a bad way. We had been warned that the Malays in these parts were not to be trusted, and here we were in the middle of a Malay kampong, and had to be off at the first gleam of dawn. We dodged about trying to find our way through to the jungle verge, but cutting across at the back of a house a woman spotted us, crying 'Orang puteh', and we knew that the chances were considerable of the Malays either hunting us up themselves or telling the Japs of our whereabouts.

We got away, however, and found a Chinese refugee who was living with his family in a Malay house. This fellow, although dithering with nervousness, gave us some raw rice and told us how to get on to Segamat Kechik. It was something to be on the right trail again after our failure the previous day. We hurried on, full of optimism, into the jungle, but alas! the path after forking several times into woodcutters' tracks finally petered out. Our fever came on. In despair we lay up for the day in a small clearing which had been used as a dump for tree trunks as they were dragged out of the jungle by means of crude 'tramways' which Chinese employ. That evening was an agony for us both, as Elliott had developed a most terrible heat rash all over his body, and I was weak with fever. We crawled out of the jungle the way we had come and managed to beg a meal off some friendly Chinese, returning as soon as we could to sleep as Elliott's pain was too bad to allow of any further marching that night.

CHAPTER 11

BETRAYAL AND CAPTURE

27th March. Things looked very serious for us: apart from our reserve of iron rations, not to be touched except in the gravest emergency such as getting lost in the depths of the jungle, we had almost run out of provisions: we were daily becoming weaker from our attacks of malaria and if we continued as were, without quinine, we would eventually peg out. Although at the very outset I had realised I had to face this possibility, I did not like the idea at all now that it was confronting me.

We had a council of war and decided it was hopeless trying to get to Segamat Kechik in our present state. We must somehow get near civilisation and hope to obtain quinine through some friendly Chinese. Our new plan therefore was to get down to the river which we had crossed at dawn, steal a dugout and make towards the town of Segamat proper. There was plenty of risk of running up against Malays but that had to be taken.

We spent the morning in the old clearing fashioning a sort of paddle until our fever came on. Towards evening we had a meal of rice with a tin of condensed milk to give us some energy and then left the jungle by the now well-known track. My recollection of what happened subsequently is confused. I know we walked several miles, somehow missed the main river and landed up at a fairly respectable Chinese house at about 11 pm. We knocked up the occupants to ask for help and were greeted by the housewife who was kindness personified. To our delight and subsequent enjoyment she offered to kill and cook a chicken for us. So we had one of the best meals possible and set off again with fresh heart.

Lack of adequate directions, however, again handicapped us grievously. In our ignorance and impotence we retraced our steps more than once and finally followed the course of a stream which, we argued, would surely debouch into the big river sooner or later, and

79

we would know where we were.

We paddled and waded, sometimes in mud, sometimes on good sand, past Malay houses and gardens. The young moon set, but we found a dugout which we stole from near a Malay house and tried to paddle downstream. What a fantastic wild goose chase it was! Every few minutes we would run aground and have to push and pull the dugout over the sandbank: we would bump into obstructions: with next to no freeboard the wretched thing would fill at the slightest wobble and yet, soaked through and through, we pushed on into the small hours, always hoping to come to the big river. At last we could endure no more. We parked the canoe in a creek and lay like corpses to sleep on a grassy bank.

28th March. At long last our luck finally ran out. At first light we were in the act of hiding away the miserable dugout when we were caught by a hideous old Malay whose face haunts me to this day. I say hideous because he had a horribly twisted mouth and a face I will not easily forget.

This highly unwelcome person asked us where we were going and I replied, 'Just downstream,' but that did not content him, and when he told us it was his canoe we had taken it was a bit of a blow. Eventually we told more or less the truth, though we hated the sight of him, and he said he would fetch his brother and help us. Elliott held him in conversation while I disappeared on business of my own, and on my way back I met a very nice Malay whom I liked instinctively and felt I could trust. He understood about us in a moment and said we had better get out of this locality as fast as possible, but he would go back to his house and return in a quarter of an hour with some provisions for us. I mentioned Twisty Face to him and he looked grave and told me not to trust him as he was a bad lot and might give us away to the Japanese.

True to his promise he returned with rice, coffee, bananas and sugar and then pushed off, warning me again not to trust anyone here. Elliott wondered what had held me and when I told him what I had learned he said it was too bad, as he had already met the brother-in-law of Twisty Face and thought it would be all right to trust them. More important however was that he had promised to buy us enough quinine to cure our fever from the nearby village of Ulu Tenang, and Elliott had given him ten dollars for the purpose. He had also pointed out a little place where we could lie up for the day, a rough shelter, probably a refuge built in a patch of thinnish scrub. But it was with many misgivings that I accepted all this and went to lie down in the shelter offered.

A couple of hours later a party of three – Twisty Face's brother-in-law and two other relations – brought us rice, took away our water bottles and said they would return at three o'clock with quinine and boiled water. Our fever came on as usual with a colossal temperature and not a drop of water to help matters. We both endured torments of thirst. Would those Malays ever return? I know I doubted their fidelity often enough as I tossed to and fro in a state of semi-delirium. But in spite of all my fears, sure enough soon after three o'clock they came back, Twisty Face too, and to our unspeakable relief brought our bottles, twenty tablets of quinine and some bananas. Everything was fine after all! My fever left me, I broke into a sweat and before long was talking away famously to these Malays. With enough quinine to cure our malaria we thought we would soon overcome our difficulties and would be on our way upcountry again. Shortly after the Malays left us for the night with renewed promises to help us on the morrow.

At dusk, with all our fears lulled to rest, we lay down for a good night's sleep, with boots off and kit spread all around the place, when the brother-in-law came up and asked if we were asleep yet. He said he had just come from the village in haste, as Twisty Face had reported our whereabouts to the Japanese, that Jap soldiers had arrived by car in the village only a mile away and were even now at his house; we had best leave this refuge and go further into the jungle. We were dumbfounded. While scrambling into our boots and packing our kit as best we could, the old man of the family dashed up in a flat spin saying that the Japs were hard on our tracks and that we should 'lari lekas'. As we wrestled with our belongings other Malays mysteriously appeared, seized various articles of our kit, and off we set, I clutching one boot in one hand and my haversack in the other. We dashed across the stream, struck off into some rubber, then into jungle, and after some minutes came to a halt. All the Malays except the brother-in-law had disappeared and he, with a muttered surprise and saying he would come back early next morning with our kit and some food, likewise vanished.

Our wits had been absolutely addled and here we were completely in the soup. Elliott had lost a boot, haversack, parang and groundsheet. I had both boots but had lost my gas-mask case and all its precious contents, and worst of all the quinine. We debated long what we should do, whether all this was merely a ruse to put us in a defenceless position or whether Twisty Face had really betrayed us to the Japs. If either or both were true we were in a sticky position and all my horrid suspicions came to the fore again. There wasn't much choice, but anyhow we decided to take the risk and stay where we were in the hope of getting our kit back as the brother-in-law had said, and settled down to a night of chilly anxiety as best we could.

29th March. It was a good two hours after daybreak that the brother-in-law turned up, without either breakfast or kit. He told us that the Japanese had come along as soon as we had fled, had searched the place and returned disappointed. I again asked him to bring our kit, and also to try and get more quinine, for which I gave him a further ten-dollar note. He promised to do so and said he would bring more food too.

Meanwhile another young fellow came up and stayed talking to us while the other went away. Was he just a decoy? After a long time the brother-in-law returned, but suspiciously without breakfast or our kit, saying he would get that shortly. But he had brought what he said were quinine tablets. There were only a dozen of them and a bottle of malaria mixture, but since the tablets were stamped 'Howard' I thought the chances were that they were merely a well-known brand of aspirin.

Elliott was sitting with his back to a tree and I was facing him, so he did not notice six or seven Malays who came up the path in single file behind him. I scented trouble instinctively and got on my feet, and then the Malays closed on us with a wild rush. Elliott was sat on in a couple of seconds but I, very ill-advisedly, tried desperately to resist and knocked two of the Malays down. The brother-in-law joined in the mêlée, took a stick and whacked me over the head and shoulders — but I scarcely felt it. Simultaneously a beastly rat of a Malay wearing the Jap policeman's armlet drew his parang and crying, 'Oh, so you want to try boxing, do you?' rushed upon me to deliver a downward blow on my head. I must have dodged slightly for I only got a gash about two inches above my left ear which knocked me off my feet. The game was up and I cried out that I would not resist further, but nevertheless the treacherous policeman struck me again on my right shin before he put up his parang. Then I was duly sat upon by my captors who displayed an intense savagery in their features. Twisty Face was in the background, I noticed.

When our captors saw the blood streaming over my face and clothes I think they got a bit frightened. They took a sock from my haversack, slapped it on my head and bound it up with a bandage which Elliott produced. Then still with our hands tied behind our backs, they searched us most thoroughly. An unpleasant fellow, a Malay in a white suit, evidently full of hate and glad to be able to lord it over the white man, was foremost in the searching. I ground my teeth when he abstracted my precious sheath-knife. They took Elliott's watch. I was feeling pretty rocky as the result of my head wound and it was a miserable procession through the trees, into the rubber and so to the outskirts of the kampong. We stopped at one house where they allowed Elliott to make a better job on my head with a Field Dressing, first dolloping on iodine which the Malays produced. With a further bandage on top of this the bleeding eventually stopped. Then they untied our hands and took us to the kampong of Ulu Tenang, the very place we had been so anxious to avoid.

It was only a matter of time before the Japs arrived in a car from Labis some seven miles distant, but before they came we were given a decent meal in an Indian eating shop and were allowed a tin of our own bully and a tin of milk to put in our coffee. Not long after, my usual bout of fever came on and I remember sitting rather forlornly on the grass verge by the roadside, shivering violently from head to foot from my rigor while a curious mob of onlookers crowded round.

We both fully expected to be shot on being handed over to the Japs and I jealously hung on to those last minutes as we drove down to Labis, looking to the hills that fringed the horizon for help and inspiration to buoy me up in the hour of trial. Instead of summary death however we learned on our arrival at Labis police station that we would be sent to Kuala Lumpur where there were already a number of European prisoners.

We were surprised to be treated with some sympathy, being offered cigarettes, bananas and even eggs by both natives and Japanese. One Chinese who saw that I was suffering from fever gave me two quinine tablets. Oddly enough we were not very closely guarded, but we were placed right in front of the police station and of course had to endure the gaze of the crowds all through that long trying day. In the late afternoon we were taken up in a soldiers' bus, crowded with men of all ranks, to Gemas, where for two nights we were lodged with Indian POWs in some old police barracks. They were extremely kind and did all in their power to help us in our misfortunes. Elliott tried to get medical attention for me, but the Japs said they had no doctors of their own at Gemas and I would have to wait until I got to Kuala Lumpur.

31st March. At seven in the morning we left Gemas by bus, stopped for a while at Tampin and later for a meal at Seremban. As we paused near the market I was greatly touched when a Chinese came up and surreptitiously passed me a soft meat 'pauh' or bun still warm from the nearby stall. After a long delay caused apparently by some hitch over getting petrol we were brought on the last stage of this journey by public bus, in the company of another European named Wynne who had been in a guerilla patrol behind the Japanese lines and had been 'picked up' at Port Dickson. It had been a long day and it was not until dusk that we reached Kuala Lumpur. In the former Robinson Building we had to answer routine questions and give all our particulars, all very polite and courteous, and soon after were taken away by truck. Yes, as I had feared, it was in front of the gates of Pudu Gaol that our truck drew up. It was an ending but also a beginning.

CHAPTER 12

LESSONS IN CO-PROSPERITY

Surprising as it may seem, I have, on the whole, very happy memories of my first year in prison. Apart from the early weeks of 1942 when conditions in the gaol were terrible, we seem to have managed to mix a lot of fun and real enjoyment in with the privations, the work parties, the inevitable bouts of sickness and above all the wonderful comradeship which can flourish in adversity. There was hardly a time so tough that we could not turn it into a joke with our captors providing the laughing stock.

At the end of August there was a great to-do over a Japanese order that every man was to give his parole not to escape. That any British POW had to sign such a document was an unheard-of thing, and although we could salve our conscience because we were under duress, we put up a strong resistance through our commanding officers. Eventually it came to a showdown when the officers, numbering over a hundred, refused to sign and were herded into four small cells in what had formerly been the female ward of the prison. There they remained for over four days in conditions which, if not on a level with the Black Hole of Calcutta, were at any rate in that tradition.

These fellows in their restricted space could not all sit down together, let alone lie down, and, as some were suffering from dysentery, conditions soon became quite awful. But morale remained high. Batmen contrived to smuggle in eggs, bananas and cigarettes concealed in the tubs of rice, and the guards would blandly look on while the empties were taken away littered with shells, peel and the scraps of other items. Sanitation was difficult, but the men were allowed to use a bucket in the corridor after summoning the guard by the necessary cry of 'benjo'. So they made a song about it to the well-known tune 'One man went to mow, went to mow a meadow' — as emended by the small changes of 'go', 'benjo' and 'bog' — to the evident amusement of the Jap guards and the delight of the mass of POWs in the yard beneath. The only person who really objected to this display was the guard commander whose sleep was disturbed and who requested that the prisoners should make less noise!

In the early days the POWs, initially some 400 in number, had been crowded into a small compound about fifty yards square. After six weeks practically all the available space outside the building was occupied by latrine pits. As may be imagined dysentery quickly becomes public enemy number one in such a situation, and this together with semi-starvation resulting from the low rice diet with weak vegetable water brought a continual toll of deaths.

The hospital, such as it was, was initially a shambles. In those early days, because of my malaria, I was admitted for three spells of about a week each; the first occasion was terrible and I will never forget the awful scene when, amid the stench and chaos, a half-demented patient who refused to eat kept throwing himself off his stretcher on to the stone floor.

Things soon improved however. Part of a field ambulance unit with two medical officers came into the gaol, and a padre too, a certain Captain Duckworth of whom more later. Between them all a tremendous change for the better came over the whole camp: concessions one by one were wrung from the Japs; we were allowed to extend our quarters into other parts of the prison; we had better washing facilities; and we even got some pork added to our menu — carcases that had survived in the Kuala Lumpur Cold Storage in spite of electricity cuts. From that time on, in the gaol at any rate, we never looked back.

By the time Elliott and I arrived in Pudu Gaol in April 1942 the number of POWs totalled around 800, of whom some dozens were Malayan Volunteers, and those of us who were not officers had the good fortune to be put in with the Australian company, a mixed bunch of some 150 men of the AIF. I cannot speak too highly of these Aussies: they were extremely friendly from the start and always ready to help. If I was sick they would wash my clothes, fetch my food, fill my water bottle, have a yarn: anything to soften the trial of captivity. I made many fine friends at that time, farmers from the outback of Victoria and New South Wales, bank clerks from the cities, a journalist from Melbourne and in particular a law student from Sydney named Russell Braddon. Among the Volunteers one Stanley Smith, a planter from Perak, became my special friend who nursed me devotedly through my periodic attacks of fever.

My head wound healed more or less in six weeks although the scar gave me continual irritation, and in two months I was well enough to be discharged finally from the hospital. Then came my first treat. It was the day after my birthday and I was allowed an afternoon outside the four grim walls which had been my only horizon for the past nine weeks.

For some while now the Japs had conceded us the privilege of working the gaol garden outside the walls, and every day for a couple of hours a small party was allowed to cultivate what had once been quite a flourishing market-garden under the previous regime. We laboriously cleared ground cover, lallang grass mostly, and at first confined ourselves to planting sweet potatoes; then as we acquired seeds we branched out into beans, cucumbers, spinach, etc. which, even if they did not provide the kitchen with much, at least gave us the excuse for indulging in a very pleasant form of exercise, opportunities for buying cakes and fruit through the wire by the railway at the bottom of the garden, and also – so vital to our morale – news of what was going on in the world outside. On my first occasion I was too weak to work: I just went to stretch my legs, to rejoice in the wonderful taste of freedom ('Say, you: just keep an eye on the Jap guard over there!') and to feel that thrill of excitement at the vision of the distant hills and the splash of colour from those Tamil girls walking down the road!

Out of the really terrible conditions existing in Pudu Gaol at the beginning of the Japanese time, order was gradually introduced from sheer necessity through the discipline imposed by our own officers headed by an Indian Army Brigadier as C.O. The policy of our captors was to allow POWs to organise their own affairs subject to the overriding authority of the Japanese commandant. Basic rations of rice, etc. were provided, supposedly on the scale of a Japanese soldier. Beyond that everything had to be won by negotiation between our commanding officer and the Japanese administration. Everything to do with internal admin was our concern: allocation of space, cooking, sanitation, hospital needs, 'canteen' purchases, recreation and entertainment and – immensely important throughout this awful time – the organisation of church services and other morale-boosting efforts. Conditions of course varied greatly from camp to camp and much would depend on the nature and character of the commandant and his interpreter if any. In camps where we had a Japanese-speaking officer who could stand up to the commandant and put our case with dignity, things could be markedly better.

On the Church side we were blessed by the presence of the Church of England padre I have mentioned above, Noël Duckworth, a charismatic little man who in his day had been cox of the Cambridge Eight. With his persuasive manner and marvellous sense of humour he was able to secure us many concessions. Over a period of several months Padre Duckworth was (quite amazingly) allowed to leave the gaol every day and go about his business in the town unattended. I believe he wore a white cassock to distinguish himself from other POWs and the local people would recognise him for what he was. Each day he would go 'shopping' and return with a pack bulging with tins or fruit to supplement the diet of the sick. On one occasion when I was recovering from a bout of malaria he dropped in to cell 226 and insisted on my having a tin of powdered milk. It is one of those gifts which can never be repaid, quite without price in that situation.

Besides helping sick and wounded in this kind of way and holding dynamic Sunday services in the prison yard, Duckworth proposed the formation of a prayer fellowship. This was to meet once a week in the narrow room by the main gate, set aside and furnished as a chapel, and also to support members individually through intercessory prayer during the days between. We made a list of prayer requests contributed by each person, and in this way I was introduced to the simplicity and the mystery and, dare I say it, the effectiveness of this faltering step of faith. I suppose there were a dozen or so sick men, some Australians too among us. We may have been babes in this kind of thing, but God is great, and for me this resulted in my complete freedom from malarial attacks for the following eighteen months.

As I recovered my strength I began to take part in the different activities of the gaol, learning Dutch with one of the two Dutch airmen who had been shot down near Muar in Johore, joining in the entertainments run by the Australians, helping to run the choir for Padre Duckworth and eventually taking one or two evening services for him. If there was one thing in which we were particularly lucky it was books, thanks to the policy of our captors! In the early days we were frequently sent out to clean up European houses in the town for occupation by officers and these jobs provided us with many splendid opportunities for obtaining books which, as they were of no interest to the Japanese, we were allowed to bring back with us. The Victoria Institution (a secondary school) yielded us a magnificent selection, as also did the house of a cultured Chinese named Loke Wan To, who had been educated at Cambridge and had an excellent taste in literature. With such material as this to hand we were never short of first rate books.

My difficulty was that by August my eyes began to come under strain and showed the first signs of malnutrition. For nearly three months I was able to do scarcely any reading: my eyes watered all day long, especially in the bright sunlight, and I was forced to wear a patch over my left eye which was particularly weak. Later on my vision actually became blurred and for a short time I saw everything double. Many other folk were in a similar case, some contracting ulcers and calcification of the cornea, and one man actually losing the sight of an eye. I was saved from such things by the eventual improvement of our diet by the addition of eggs which we were able to buy through our 'canteen' in considerable quantities in September.

Talking of bringing back books found in European houses reminds me of some of the tasks which the Japs set us to do. Almost every day working parties of varying numbers were required. The Japs would give the figures and leave it to the camp administration to arrange the rest. For example there were always parties going out regularly to the 'Car Park', to one or other of the ammunition dumps outside the town, to the General Hospital (to remove blast walls), to the 'school' (a government school turned into a supply depot), to the railway station or to the engine works, and we would expect to have our turn at each one.

In the early days there were plenty of opportunities for getting canned stuff and frequently men would be given presents by the Chinese; but latterly there was little to be had, unless the Japs gave a 'presento' of a can of fruit between six or seven and some cigarettes as a reward for overtime or a heavy job well done.

We would leave the gaol at about 8 am, march or go by truck to the job and get back at 7 pm, having had nothing all day except a small loaf of Chinese bread and a tin of meat or fish shared among five men. If we were fortunate we might have what was left over from the Japanese cookhouse, or be able to buy some fruit and cakes from Malay hawkers. Sometimes the work was grindingly heavy as when shifting ammunition. On other occasions we might loaf around all day long and be bored stiff with nothing to occupy us.

We came across all types of Japanese, good and bad. It was at the Car Park that the most brutal lot hung out: here we would have to knock broken-down vehicles to pieces or attempt to repair others, in momentary expectation of a bashing for some imagined offence. We would be thoroughly searched too, and would get unmercifully beaten if anything pilfered was found. I remember one occasion when some salt had been put out to dry: so obviously that most chaps took it to be a bait and avoided it! One Australian was rash enough to pinch a handful. Well, when we were lined up for the search the Japs went through our haversacks, looking for one thing: salt. Everything else — wire, screws, nails, wood, paper, etc. — was ignored, but the chap in whose bundle the salt was found was beaten and kicked quite horribly in front of us all.

One thing that the Japs always respected was our religious activities and we were allowed to hold church services all along. As I have mentioned we were given a little room by the main gate as a chapel. Although it could not seat more than thirty with comfort, scores of fellows used to crowd into it in the evenings at the regular services held by the padre and, when there was a talk or a brains trust on, humanity would stream outside in order to be able to listen. The plain whitewashed walls were decorated with the badges of the various units in the camp, beautifully executed in black and white by one of the officers. There was a simple altar and lectern too, both made in the gaol workshops.

Within the four walls of the gaol, entertainments flourished to a wonderful degree. On Saturday nights there would be a full-dress show in the central court, on a stage erected by the Engineers, and the different companies in turn would put on Variety, always popular with the Japanese. One of our girl impersonators was so convincing that after a certain performance a Jap came backstage to investigate the reality of the illusion! I was caught up in one of the sketches in the Australian show, playing the part of a mill-girl with a red handkerchief over my hair and red chalk over my cheeks and lips: but I may have been rather thinner then. Altogether this particular show was voted an outrageous success, especially the ballet scene where the pick of our youth frolicked shamelessly with bosoms adorned with halves of coconut shells. A five-man dance band supplied the music.

One morning in the middle of August the whole gaol was electrified to learn that two parties had escaped in the night, one of seven and a smaller one of three, both organised and led by Volunteer officers. I had known that certain people were fomenting plans for escape for a considerable period because Elliott was involved in them and he had asked me if I would like to join him again, but when the combined break was made it came as a complete surprise to most of us.

You may well wonder how the attempt was made, and indeed the whole affair is as remarkable as any fiction. The officer at the head of the bigger party had got a key made to one of the postern gates of the gaol, and for weeks beforehand had been in the habit of slipping out at night to make his contacts and complete the arrangements for the escape. I gathered that all the different parties had coordinated their plans so as to make their attempts on the same night. A date had been set, but for some reason or other the two parties which got away anticipated it by a week and left without letting the other parties know: hence Elliott, among others, was stranded, highly enraged at being double-crossed. We covered up the absences of the ten individuals for twenty-four hours, and when the Japs eventually got wind of what had happened they could not believe their ears. The little clerk who used to come round to our roll call was greatly tickled by the whole affair, and secure in his own position laughed and chuckled as he counted and re-counted our parade. The episode however ended tragically for all concerned. In a matter of days we learned that all the men had been recaptured, the larger group having got in touch with Chinese guerillas who had done their best to save them from the Japs. A pitched battle was fought with several casualties and a whole village was subsequently wiped out as a reprisal. The escapees were all brought back to the gaol, strictly segregated, and a few weeks later we were forced to conclude from circumstantial evidence that they had been taken away and executed.

CHAPTER 13

A FILM FOR NIPPON

At the end of September 1942 the camp began to break up. Two large parties of sick were taken down to Singapore, a party of 400 went North to Thailand and then all the Australians went South, leaving only a hundred men in the gaol including half a dozen Volunteers. This small party, we were told, was to proceed to Singapore by stages and was to be used for the making of a film about the Malayan campaign. As things turned out, the experience proved most interesting, and I was glad I had been included in the party.

We spent a further month in the gaol, going out every fine day to a spot some five miles outside the town near the village of Ampang. Here, in the neighbourhood of some old Chinese tin-workings, the filming took place, and although it involved a lot of hanging around with nothing to do for much of the time we did get quite a deal of fun out of the procedure. The incident being filmed here portrayed British troops defending a hill from trenches, while the glorious soldiers of Nippon attacked in force, eventually winning the position. At the summit a sham house had been constructed whose demolition was to be the climax of this part. A great quantity of lime had been stacked in the building to help the illusion of the explosion which, when it happened, caused considerable excitement as one Jap together with an unfortunate coolie were blown up too.

In the middle of November we were taken down to Malacca by truck. It was a tremendous thrill to leave the gaol at last after nearly eight months inside, and we were a very lively party as we set off clinging to the top of our kit in our three lorries. We did the eighty miles in a leisurely fashion, and were allowed to stop in Seremban where we all piled into a coffee shop at the side of the road. But for me the greatest moment of the day was when we rolled into the village of Alor Gajah and drew up by the shop-houses fronting the

93

padang. We were to have a five-minute halt for a cup of coffee. I alighted from the truck and looked around. A crowd had quickly gathered but I could not spot anyone familiar to me out of that sea of faces, when a Malay kid, the one I remembered who had pulled the punkah for me in Court, spotted me and called out my name. I climbed on to the side-walk as if to go into one of the shops, but before I could get inside I was surrounded by a crowd of people with everybody trying to shake me by the hand and firing questions at me nineteen to the dozen.

What sort of view, I wondered, would the Japs take of this display of interest and affection by their newly-conquered subjects? When the interpreter strolled across I was feeling distinctly nervous. However, after a question or two, he said, to my amazement, that he had no objection to my talking to these people, and then left me to enjoy one of the most glorious five minutes of my life.

Someone ran across to the District Office to call the clerks over to meet me, while another went to summon the Malay who had formerly been my munshi. The old policeman who had been my court orderly protested his loyalty with tears in his eyes and said that it was only to earn a livelihood for himself and his family that he continued to work under the Japanese. My old teacher came up in an old white suit, looking much the worse for wear and also very much thinner. He said that although the vernacular school was still open he had been thrown out of his job and that the lot of schoolmasters such as he (ex-Volunteers I suppose) was very hard.

I saw the Tamil clerk too, a rascally-looking fellow called Doraisamy: he told me the news about the District Office which was working at about half-pressure and gave me details of various people I asked about. But then the word was given that we were about to move off. I hastily drank the glass of lemonade that had been thrust into my hand and scrambled on to the tail of my truck among shouts of goodwill from all. The one person I missed was Ranting, my former cook-boy. I was told he was now a seller of 'sati' and doing quite well.

After this rousing welcome at Alor Gajah it was rather an anti-climax to arrive at Malacca and be taken straight to the gaol. In the palmy days of peace I had been there several times, but in the capacity of Visiting Justice: now the tables were turned and I felt the irony of the situation. However we found we were in luck, as the gaol was being run by a Eurasian, Mr Marbeck, a former Hospital Dresser very friendly to the Europeans. We gathered that he had already done a lot for some Australian soldiers as well as civilians who had happened to land up in his custody. This gaol was really tiny, and was already full of prisoners, many of them Chinese taken in on charges of working against the Japanese, but one building was cleared for us and we were squashed in, I and five others occupying the space under the hangman's drop! The Japanese officer in charge left us entirely in the hands of the local people, with the result that we were treated royally and fed on the best that the town and the gaol could provide. In addition the Eurasian community made a collection for us, and we were presented with half a dozen fowls for the pot as well as bananas and cigarettes.

Malacca was a little oasis. Quite untroubled by Japs for a few days we were able to make friends with some of the civilian prisoners. These were young Eurasian boys of Portuguese descent, with names like Texeiro or Fernandez, who had been pulled into the gaol on trivial charges. From them I learned how to grind chillie with ginger root and other ingredients for curry and so make the most of the raw material we might have in the cookhouse.

Here we remained for ten days, going out two or three times to take part in some filming. On one of these occasions we went out to the former Volunteer camp at Tanjong Kling, now pretty well wrecked, and did some beach scenes. Afterwards we were allowed to have a swim, a great privilege at such a time. It was at the very spot where Louise and I had spent our last hour together before I was sent down to take part in the defence of Singapore.

The producers of the film wanted to shoot some scenes at Parit Sulong, a village some fifteen miles south of Muar, in Johore, where a big action had taken place in the course of the campaign. Here an Australian battalion had been ambushed and had suffered tremendous losses, and when we came to the spot we found the roadside still littered with the remains of crashed and burned-out vehicles.

We spent several days at this village, coming out each morning from Muar where, of course, we were lodged in the gaol. We were filmed defending the bridge over the river, and had to retreat before the advance of the superior Japanese. We did not at all like the idea of doing anything that suggested cowardice and several times our officer lodged protests when we were directed to do something that appeared particularly odious to us. A compromise was reached whereby the Japanese agreed not to make us perform any action which would reflect disgracefully on British valour. Eventually our officers skilfully carried out a rearguard action in which our men continued retreating while firing up to the last minute, a display which satisfied both parties. During one of the scenes in a scrubby patch of ground a young wild pig was found, and after an exciting chase was shot by one of our guards. We were presented with the carcase and so had the pleasure of living on pork for the next two days.

The last stop for us on this curious journey was Johore Bahru, at the southernmost tip of the Peninsula, and here we remained for an extremely wet and uncomfortable fortnight in the gaol there. The weather was too bad for any filming and we became distinctly bored cooped up inside the dreary place for so long. Moreover the food was bad and the rations quite miserable. The cells were alive with bugs which gave us no rest at night and we were so hungry that I remember now with shame covertly picking over the refuse bins. What a relief when, three days before Christmas 1942, we crossed the Causeway and were taken to join the bulk of the British POWs in the former Army barracks at Changi.

For me the most interesting part of the trip lay in the opportunities I had of meeting and talking with Chinese and Malays, and I was able to form a fair idea of how these people were reacting to the Japanese occupation. In Johore Bahru gaol, for instance, I made friends with a Malay warder who was from my old district of Alor Gajah. He told me about conditions in the kampongs, of Japanese depredations, of the tithing of all rice grown. Whatever the view of the Malays in the early days of the war, there was no doubt they would now have given a great deal to have the British back again.

These six weeks, during which we had been able to see quite a bit of the Malayan countryside and had enjoyed a measure of freedom denied to the majority of POWs, had been altogether a most pleasant break from the monotony of prison life. All the same, we were glad to get back to our fellows at Changi, and to feel that we were once again members of a large community with its wider interests and contacts.

CHAPTER 14

THE RAILROAD OF DEATH

The Japanese Emperor had ordered the construction of the Bangkok-Moulmein railway line. It was an essential link in the line of communications for the Imperial Japanese Army in Burma, to maintain the troops there after the successful drive in 1942, and to enable the build-up necessary for the great offensive against India. The railway line was to be driven through in the minimum of time, in the face of monsoon conditions and regardless of the cost in human lives.

As early as September 1942, reports of this task had trickled through the walls of Pudu Gaol, and before the end of the month, as recounted earlier, a party of the fittest men, numbering 400, had been selected to proceed North by rail. This was but one small unit out of hundreds which were drawn from prison camps all over the Netherlands East Indies as well as from Singapore itself.

From Changi several thousands of POWs of all nationalities had already left for Thailand and Burma before I got down there at Christmas time. We lived in daily expectation of being detailed for a move. We all longed for change, it may be true, but at the same time we preferred the devil we knew, and distrusted the enticing promises of the Japs. We were encouraged to believe that we were going to rest camps: we were to take unfit men with us, for in Thailand there would be more food and a better climate. All we would have to do would be to build our own camps and look after ourselves! F and H forces which left Changi in April and May 1943 not only took equipment for camp construction, plumbing etc, but also a whole outfit for camp entertainment, medical services and so on. The grim realities which we experienced mocked these optimistic and elaborate preparations.

At the beginning of 1943 I spent four peaceful months in Changi barracks area, living the sheltered life of batman to Padre Petter,

Chaplain to the Malacca Volunteers, whom Louise and I had got to know during our time at Alor Gajah and liked enormously. He was in his sixties, I believe, and white-haired, but because of his down-to-earth manner and uproarious sense of humour he was a popular character and many people sought his company. In this situation, sharing quarters with a number of FMS Volunteers in a garage belonging to an officer's house, I was well content with a placid way of life with its minor duties after the turmoil and privations of the past twelve months.

There were excellent opportunities for reading and study — a kind of open university had been established in the camp — and wonderful entertainments to prevent the evenings from dragging. At this time I was taught how to knit by a Singapore Volunteer called John Walters (Chartered Bank) and made my first socks from wool taken from army hosetops. In later days I made good use of this new skill, and it certainly helped to keep me sane during the trying months ahead.

Towards the end of February I was admitted to the camp hospital because of some concern over my head wound, and after consultations with top specialists I had a minor operation to tidy up the damage. This was performed by one of the King's physicians, Col. Sir Julian Taylor. He did a thorough job under a regional anaesthetic, scraping away broken bone and excising the old scar. In a few days I was pronounced fit and told that it would not trouble me again.

Besides being a rest and a cure my time in hospital enabled me to make a number of new friends: a Dutch lad from Sumatra, a sailor in the Dutch Navy, in for an intricate nerve-graft: a Scot, Pipe-Corporal Johnstone, of the Gordons, who had nearly had his left arm severed when he avoided the blow of a Samurai's sword which was meant to decapitate him. This brave man had escaped from Changi, and was on the point of being summarily executed on his recapture when he made that last bid for his life and won it so incredibly. He dived into the Straits and was in the water for five hours before he was picked up: it was a miracle he did not bleed to death.

Another patient, a merchant seaman, told me of his capture by a

German raider in the Indian Ocean: for several months he was in a prison ship until his recent transfer to less humane Japanese in Singapore. Beside all these I had my old friends, colleagues in the Malayan Civil Service, for instance Len Morrison and John Peel who were always good company and became firm friends. There were also those splendid Australians who had looked after me so well in Pudu Gaol, but gradually most of the these dropped out of circulation in Singapore: some were taken to Japan, some to Borneo, but the majority were drafted 'upcountry', the euphemism for the unknown North. The camp was beginning to break up, the numbers reduced to a fraction of its former 50,000 odd. The Japanese had a priority task to accomplish in Thailand, and moreover it was an increasingly hard problem to feed so many mouths on the Island.

In the beginning of May 1943 I was picked with some 60 other Volunteers to join a body of mixed English units, which was to form Party 5 of 'H' Force under the command Lt. Col. H.P. Newey, formerly the C.O. of the Straits Settlements Volunteers. He was the one, you may remember, who had given me field punishment in Singapore in the early days of the war. Well, we had our 'shots', typhoid, dysentery and plague, packed huge kits, and in the early morning of 13th May were taken by truck to Singapore Station. I should explain that 'H' Force totalled 3,600, comprising six parties of 600 each. ('F' force, whose history in Thailand was even more notorious than ours, was similarly organised.) One officer per 100 men was allowed together with a doctor and a small cadre of medical personnel. The last of the parties, H6, consisted entirely of officers. So urgently did the Japanese require labour that they did not scruple to use these officers on the same level as other ranks: they had, in fact, been inveigled into the Force on the understanding that they would only be required to officer troops, to help in the camps where there might be a shortage of officers, and so on. Of course it did not work out like that and they became slave labour like the rest. I must confess, however, that when it came to the point it did give me some satisfaction to be working side by side for example with a major in the Indian Army. Hitherto most officers had in the main been fairly sheltered while the men seemed to get the dirty end of the stick. Our shared experience in Thailand evened things up a bit.

Our first ordeal was the four-day train journey from Singapore to Banpong in Thailand, a distance of some 1,200 miles. For this we were crammed 27 to a steel-sided covered wagon with all our kit. By day the heat was intense, and by night there was no room to stretch out — we could only sit on our packs, our heads nodding against each other, intermittently dozing through the jarring and rattling of the rolling stock. We were given two meals a day, rice with a watery vegetable stew or a piece of dried salt fish, and we stopped on the way fairly frequently, often being able to buy cakes and fruit from the Malays at the stations. We used to beg boiling water from the Eurasian railway drivers with which to make tea: as it came out scalding we presumed it was safe for us to drink! Sometimes we got a wash under one of those big pumps meant for the use of the engines, and then all you could see would be a scrum of naked bodies good-humouredly scrapping to get under the improvised shower!

For me all this was not so unbearable as the above account might indicate. For one thing I had secured a place by the opening provided by the sliding door, and was able to enjoy the breeze. Furthermore I was in a truck of Volunteers and assorted units, and found plenty of interest in making new friends. One to whom I became particularly attached was a young lad of twenty-three, named Teddie Wolfe. He had been through the Dunkirk campaign as a gunner in one of the Territorial regiments — and now this. We soon struck up a friendship which although short-lived helped us through a lot in the following days. You could say it was the happiest thing I possessed at the time, and it was just too bad when he fell victim to cholera some two months later.

The real scramble started at Banpong, the town some 100 miles to the West of Bangkok, from which the projected railway was to wriggle out like some formless snake through the virgin jungle, over the passes of Upper Siam, and so through to Burma by the Three Pagodas Pass. We detrained and staggered a mile through the town under the weight of our heavy kits to our transit camp, a huddle of long, high-roofed bamboo huts inside a muddy compound. Here we spent two days, resting, getting clean, selling some of our surplus clothing to the Thais for ticuls (Thai dollars) so essential to us for the purchase of food. Eggs and fruit of all sorts were abundant: it was wonderful after the semi-famine conditions of Singapore, and many fellows ate unwisely, contracting diarrhoea and worse, a bad start for the marathon which lay ahead. So keen were the Thais on acquiring our khaki clothing that we were pestered to part with our last garment at the bathing place, and I was obliged to remonstrate with a Thai woman who tried to steal my shorts through the bamboo fence while I was in the very act of bathing!

At Singapore we had been assured we would have transport to our camps. But here it was a very different story, for although the new line was working for a distance of some 60 miles, we were for some unknown reason not able to get a ride all the way. So with considerable reservations we were forced to leave our heavy kit to the tender mercies of the local guard of Dutch conscripts, and swung off at about 10 pm on the first stage of the 35 mile march. By dawn we had covered 16 miles, and a sorry lot it was which straggled in to the school which was our halting place. The pace of the march and the distance had proved too much for many of the men, already unfit and now further weakened by the rigours of the journey, by ill-fitting boots and in many cases by diarrhoea. The march, a trivial affair in normal times, was the beginning of our misfortunes, for it broke many of the men before ever they got to the really heavy work on the railway: ulcers, for example, contracted in the first few days, contributed to the death of scores before many weeks were out.

It was the usual practice of the Japs to make us march by night. By the morning of the second day, when we crawled in to the transit camp at Kanburi, exhausted from the all-night march and lack of sleep, we were dead beat and slept solidly through the day, under bushes, shrubs, anything that would provide shelter. In another party two Dutchmen who had neglected to ensure that they were in the shade died of sunstroke. We had only some half dozen small tents with us for the whole 600 men and when it came on to rain in torrents in the evening our situation could hardly have been more miserable. Teddie Wolfe and I found a refuge under the eaves of a nearby house, while many POWs sneaked across to a kampong and begged shelter from the Thais. Others attempted to rig bivouacs from their groundsheets and got soaked. To give him credit our C.O. did all he could with the Japs, and on the following day we were allowed to cram ourselves into two huts in a neighbouring camp. My pitch then, for two night, was *under* the sleeping platform, affording a clearance of two feet. But we had two meals a day, were able to wash and were allowed to buy food from a canteen run for the Japs by the local Thais. So far things could have been a lot worse: we kept up our spirits and passed the days of waiting before moving up the line in reading, sleep and rest.

CHAPTER 15

TONCHAN

Trains were now running as far as a big advanced base camp called Tarso, 30 or 40 miles on, and we were lucky enough to get a lift all that way on bogey trucks loaded with rails. Straddled across these hard objects, we endured the journey through the heat of the day, travelling for the most part through dull sparse jungle. We had one thrill, however, when the line clung desperately to the edge of a precipice hundreds of feet above a raging torrent, and then crawled in a fantastic curve across the abyss by a wooden trestle bridge on concrete foundations. We could only hold our breath and pray that no derailment would occur. Our nerves were not in the best of shape!

We eventually arrived at the site of our first camp at 2 am on the following morning after a terrible night trek through the jungle. The distance from Tarso to our camp could not have been more than six or seven miles, but the way was along a miry track, agonisingly heavy going and causing many falls. Being entirely shut in by jungle trees we got no light from the stars. Rain fell, off and on. Fortunately I still had a change of dry clothes, a groundsheet and a mosquito net, so things could have been a lot worse. We were given one day in which to clear the jungle and build our camp and we set to at first light with surprising zeal and cheerfulness. The sun shone and the brightness of the day gave some colour to our hopes. Perhaps things would not turn out so badly and anyway we did, at least, now have a canvas shelter over our heads, even if we were forty to a tent designed for a quarter of that number.

H force had been detailed to share, with forces of Chinese, Tamil and Malay labour, the construction of a certain stretch of line, and the different groups were scattered in camps of 200 or 300 men at intervals along the route. I remained at the first camp for a month, and in that time worked on building embankments, digging out and carrying the scheduled amount of one cubic metre of earth a day: then on making a cutting, where one either used a hammer and drill to prepare for blasting or else cleared rock and debris that had already been blasted. The worst was bridge-building, as this meant manhandling huge logs into position, twenty or thirty men to a log, and a false move or a foot wrong could mean a fall into the stream or swamp below, or result in being crushed by a rolling log. I recall a man in the Signals who had had to have a leg amputated for that reason. I saw him a few times in our hospital hut, but heard later that he had died of gangrene.

A typical day at Tonchan would be something like this: we would be up and eating our breakfast of 'pap rice' by dawn. Work parade would follow immediately, tools would be collected and off we would trudge in different parties to the task. The cutting we were working on was a good three miles from the camp and a tiring trek along a deeply-rutted track, then through scrub and thin jungle until we came to the line which scored its way inexorably through everything. In the course of the day's work we would be given a quarter of an hour's smoko, when we could get a mug of boiled water or tea if we were lucky, an hour for tiffin and another break in the course of the afternoon. Work would stop at about five or six o'clock depending on the amount done, and whether the Japs decided to blast or not. Then the tremendous relief of being free from the slavery for a few hours, a great rush to get back to camp as quickly as possible and then, if there was time before supper, a wash in the little river that ran through the camp. The privilege of bathing, however, was not to be ours for long. The rains had already set in for some weeks now, and we had not been at Tonchan a week before the dreaded scourge of cholera broke out in our midst.

The trouble had started in the Tamil camp which bordered ours, and spread like wild-fire owing to the insane policy of the Japanese. The Tamils were camped upstream from us, and it was notorious that they would use running water whenever they could for any purpose, including that of relieving nature. We too had to use this water, polluted as it was, both for the kitchen and for washing. Before we became aware that an epidemic had broken out, men began going down right and left. Then, of course, the Japs ordered all due precautions. All water had to be boiled, all cholera cases isolated. They themselves were scared stiff by the nature of the disease and caused us much amusement by the way they went about with medicated gauze over their mouths and noses, spraying themselves with cresol at every opportunity. They would never handle a corpse: that was a job for POWs, and apart from a wash or a spray with antiseptic we would get no protective treatment. One thing however I should mention: while at Kanburi we had been given a cholera injection which may have helped to immunise some of us. But we did not have much faith in Japanese serums.

One amusing incident occurred on the very day that the cholera broke out. I was working on a fatigue, fetching bamboos into the camp, when I met a party from another British camp that was just across the road and was puzzled by the familiar appearance of a wild-looking red-bearded fellow. I was just wondering who he was when he startled me by saying in a very urbane voice: 'Hello, Geof: nice to see you here!' It was my cousin Tony Loch, a fellow Volunteer and also Malayan Civil Servant, who had gone North from Singapore in October 1942 and had been in Thailand ever since. He had had a bad attack of rheumatic fever and had only just scraped through it. Apart from his beard and looking very much thinner he was the same as when I last saw him some eighteen months before. He had been nursed through his illness by fellow Volunteers, among them another mutual friend, Tony Mills, whom I met subsequently on a visit to their camp.

I celebrated my 26th birthday on the cutting and remember this because I landed a bashing from one of the Jap engineers. No doubt he thought I was not working hard enough for a subject of the Emperor and of course he was right! After that I went down with an attack of enteritis and got a couple of days off work. That was a blessed rest indeed, and here the Japs were not so ruthless in driving out the sick to work as they were to become later on, but then the number of fit men was still relatively high. While I was 'bed-down' in camp I got the most pleasant surprise: to my great joy my heavy pack arrived in a consignment of baggage from the base camp, a great piece of luck as only two lorry loads ever came through. Besides now having some clean clothes, razor, soap and so on, I got my previous blanket which was now absolutely essential as the nights became quite cold.

By way of light work to help my recovery I was detailed to work in the Japanese cookhouse. This was easy, but it was also monotonous and a continual strain. One had a constant craving to pilfer pieces of fish, meat, anything that happened to be around, and of course severe punishment was meted out for anything discovered. Once another chap and I were put on to sorting eggs, picking out the bad from a basket containing some two gross. We did the job and included a few good ones among our choice of bad, hoping to get away with them. In the end the Japanese cook never bothered to check the bad eggs which we later swiped, hiding them in the rubbish pit until we got the chance of removing them in our haversacks. It was wonderful what some chaps were able to get away with. Sugar, salt, sweet potatoes and bits of pork, eggs and fish all found their way back to our camp to swell our scanty suppers.

In Tonchan we had an existence that was relatively tolerable compared with that in other camps. Conditions were hard, of course, but at least we were able to look after ourselves and as the bogey of night-work had not so far been brought in we got plenty of sleep. Food was poor. For the first four weeks there was little beyond rice, dried fish and 'jungle stew', but before long our officers organised 'canteen' supplies financed from a fund brought up with us from Changi. Goods were purchased from barges plying up and down the river when tobacco, gula malacca (a kind of dark brown sugar rather like fudge), biscuits, tinned food, pig-oil, oil, etc, became available in small quantities at exorbitant prices. By the end of June we really began to get some good food, including vegetables, eggs and dried fish when the railway line was pushed right up to the boundary of the camp. As usual food was not short in Thailand: it was the problem of distribution, in a country devoid of communications apart from its rivers, which brought us to the borderline of actual starvation.

CHAPTER 16

HINTOCK RIVER

Towards the end of June 1943 we received orders to move on. The greater part of our task in the neighbourhood of Tonchan had been completed, the line was through and H5 together with H6, the officers' group which had joined forces with us, were required to find a party of 200 men to take up a site some twenty miles higher up the line. I was picked for this, but Teddie Wolfe was under the weather with a bad bout of diarrhoea at this time and so we were separated, much to my disappointment. It took us two days and a night to march to our new camp, and it was during this nightmare journey that I had the grimmest experience of my whole captivity. The first day was not too bad, although we staggered under our heavy loads – tents and cooking gear as well as our personal kit. We took turns at humping the ton-weight tents, slung on poles between two men. Worst of all were the kualis, the heavy iron cooking pans shaped like gigantic woks about four feet in diameter. The best way I found was to carry the thing upside down resting upon my head, but then one could hardly see the path ahead! Some men were too weak to take their share, hardly able to manage their own packs. Our M.O. on that march, Captain Driver, was quite wonderful, up and down the line of men with his outsize waterbottle, helping those most distressed, often to be seen carrying an extra pack.

Through endless jungle we trekked in single file, slipping, breathless, cursing, gritting our teeth and carrying on yet another hundred yards. At times we would pass a horde of Tamils or Chinese who were streaming away in scores from their cholera-stricken camps with all the pitiful paraphernalia that one associates with the Asiatic when in flight from flood, famine or war. So now these folk tottered past, many obviously on their last legs from exhaustion or sickness, still grimly hanging on to the kandar stick which held their hoard of chattels – cooking pots, sleeping mats, bottles, rags — sorry vestiges of their former existence. We had ourselves been degraded so low by this time that we could give them nothing beyond a casual stare. Like us, whether Tamils, Chinese or Malays, numbering in the region of 100,000 or more, they were pawns to be sacrificed in this vast wastage of human effort.

The evening of our first day's march we unexpectedly got some supper. An hour before dusk we reached the camp which was the Headquarters camp of H force. It was called Kanu and had been established for some time, originally for construction, but now for maintenance and as a staging post for poor devils like us. The Japs would not let us enter the camp or stop there for fear of introducing cholera, but at any rate they saw that we did at least have a meal before starting off on the night march to Hintock Jungle camp, five miles in from the river we were heading for. We ate the rations of rice and stew and rested in the blukar outside the lines, put our feet up on our packs and waited for dusk to fall and the order to move off.

We were chatting quietly among ourselves, some were smoking, some were dozing. It was the hour when the jungle trees were falling into shadow, when the cicadas began to stay their interminable churr churr and stars were coming out to prick the sky with points of silver, when from the camp there came a sound which immediately transfixed every one of us. It was a trumpet, a trumpet quite beautifully played, the notes coming with absolute distinctness and purity across the intervening distance. Someone was playing old music-hall tunes, the 'Londonderry Air' for instance, and wartime melodies like 'Far, far on the Range' and 'When they sound the last All Clear', tunes which tugged at the heartstrings with more than a touch of irony as they sounded so purely in the depths of that jungle clearing. The concert ended but there was one more thing before the unknown trumpeter broke off. It was the playing of 'Last Post', giving finality to that day, if not to us. If ever we needed light in dark places, if ever we needed encouragement in despair, if ever we needed strength which comes from fellowship, we had it then in abundance.

The word was given to move and we stiffly found our legs and teetered like blind beggars up the track which was merely a darker black than the blackness all around. Physically and morally speaking the night which followed remains in my mind as the most terrible experience of my life. Our route followed narrow jungle paths; we were in single file following a Jap N.C.O., the only person carrying a torch. In the blackness of night it was quite impossible to maintain contact without actually hanging on to the man in front. We staggered on in mud, tripping continually over tree-roots and dependent on the fellow in front for warnings like 'pothole', 'fallen tree' and so on.

I recall the Japanese guide losing the way and the frustration we felt at having to turn back to find the right track. As the night wore on and we became increasingly exhausted, the line of march became more and more spread out. Men became mutinous with exhaustion, rage and nerves. Some fell out and were left as they lay. Eventually, having completely lost the way, our Jap N.C.O. called a halt, whereupon we sank down by the side of the muddy track and slept until the dawn.

I awoke to find myself alone, with my kit and whatever I had been carrying. I took a few mouthfuls from my water bottle and knew what it was to get up and push myself forward step by step beyond the limits of endurance. As daylight broke I staggered into the camp which had been our next objective, called, I think, Kanu 2. Some fellows had arrived quite some time earlier: others trailed in over the next hour or two. But we had made it, and the cooks from the camp brought pap-rice. It was ambrosia.

Our immediate trials were not ended by our arrival at our next halting place, Hintock Jungle camp, for although we got a rest and a meal there we still had several miles of difficult country to cross, climbing over a steep escarpment before we could descend again to the river where we were to camp. The trickiest place was a spot called 'Jacob's Ladder' where the path negotiated an almost sheer cliff-face. Here a ladder of bamboos had been erected, and one by one we had to climb this rickety contraption, somehow manhandling the heavy loads as well. But the worst of this awful journey was over and we could take the rest of it fairly easily since the gradient was downhill all the way. It was about an hour before dusk when we reached the camp site. Oh, heavens, the same old story all over again: jungle to clear, the camp to build, and all this to be done in what was left of the daylight, for tomorrow we would be herded on to the new task, the blasting of a new cutting a couple of miles from the camp. Tired as we were, we cut down enough of the heavy bamboo to form the nucleus of our site. The cooks too did wonders, and before we lay down that night we did at least have a meal in our stomachs and a piece of canvas over our heads.

CHAPTER 17

ON THE CUTTING

The work on this part of the railway, based on Hintock River camp, had to be pushed through quickly, as the engineers' programme was behind schedule, and this meant that we were required to work three shifts, 8 to 4, 4 to midnight, and midnight until dawn. Our party was divided up into the necessary shifts, and I found that I was put on the 4 to midnight one, and I stuck to this for some ten days. As far as work under the Japs went, we reckoned that we did not do too badly on this shift, for darkness hides a multitude of slackers and control was not nearly so strict as by day.

We would leave the camp at about 3 o'clock in the afternoon and walk and scramble to the job by the usual muddy track. At this point the railway line clung to the side of the valley, some way above the camp, and so for the last part of the way we had to climb steeply over rocks and boulders, pushing through thickets of bamboos. This cutting was a pretty big affair, over fifty feet deep, and the procedure was the same as at Tonchan, only here the Japanese had somehow got a diesel generator and compressor up from the river which drove a couple of pneumatic drills. Twice each shift there would be a blast; we would scurry for shelter behind trees well in the background, while tons of rock and debris would go up in the air and showers of small stuff hurtle past us. From another cutting, rather nearer to the camp, rocks sometimes fell among our very tents, but I never heard of anyone being injured. We would have our evening meal before dusk and then go back to the task which would be lit by a host of carbide flares, or by flickering lights given out by pieces of sacking stuck in tins of diesel oil.

It was truly an amazing sight. Occasionally I would stand a few yards away from the circle of lights and marvel at the strange beauty of the myriad twinkling points in the depths of the surrounding blackness. I would see the little figures moving dimly about, like ants in an ant-hill, painfully clearing away the thousands of tons of rock and earth and I would feel stunned by the immensity of the task and the appalling waste of lives and effort to accomplish it. Then I would have to go back to the spot where I was grubbing up the sand and rocky chips from a hole, while a Japanese engineer, with a stick in hand, would stand over me to see that I was doing my share, and I would wait until he moved on to give his attention to some other wretched POW.

As the cutting bit deeper into the side of the hill we would lay down light rails and run small trucks to and fro, carrying the rubbish and tipping it out over the ravine which had to filled in beyond the cutting. Sometimes I would have a spell on this job which was hard work and entailed quite a bit of skill in jumping the ties and avoiding being flung over the end of the tip and down into the ravine below.

Once I had a narrow escape when I slipped and thought I was a goner, but just managed to clutch on to the framework below and got away with a minor gash on my leg. When the shift finally came to an end at midnight we would somehow have to find our way back to the camp. We would form up in groups of ten or a dozen and would be given an oil flare to light us on our way. Then it would be a scramble to see whether we could get back before the flare burned out, and one would consider oneself lucky if the trip was accomplished without a fall which would cover one in mud if no worse. And our reward? Possibly a mug of thin soup and a fried rissole before we turned in to snatch what sleep we could before daylight. I must say that on the whole this shift was popular, for it meant that one was out of the blazing sun and also had the chance of washing clothes, etc, in the morning. On the other hand it was often extremely cold, especially after rain, and I preferred to work in a shirt even if I sweated, rather than stripped to the waist and risk a chill.

After ten days I was transferred to an all-day task on another cutting, quite a different proposition from the previous work, for this was supervised by a terrible Jap who, owing to his resemblance to a certain gorilla at the Sydney Zoo, was nicknamed 'Molly'. He was big-built for a Japanese, had a brutal face and never spoke but rather

113

barked in a series of staccato bursts. His appearance was indeed terrifying, but I have to say that his behaviour as a taskmaster was not all that bad. What gave us the pip working under him was his habit of keeping up a running commentary from a rock some feet above us. From this perch, feet aggressively astride, and with a large bamboo in his hand, he would cast an eagle eye around, and woe betide any luckless man whom he caught bludging (to use a popular Australian expression).

One day some of us Volunteers were engaged in moving heavy rocks under the supervision of a wiry little engineer, one of Molly's off-siders. Six of us had gathered round a particularly nasty rock which after repeated efforts we had failed to budge, when up comes this little Jap, wearing the thin drab breeches and rubber shoes and white gloves, the usual dress of this breed, and jabbers away at us in Japanese with a few words of broken English thrown in. It is obvious he is cursing us for a lot of lousy good-for-nothings, and he will show us how the job is to be done. So he sets to, his muscles rippling all round this big chunk of rock, and after much heaving and grunting he does manage to roll the darn thing over, with us standing by, quietly interested spectators. Then he turns on us with an angry babble, seizes a stick and lays into us until his ego is satisfied and we have each received a clout, following this up with a little lecture on 'British soldier strong as Nippon soldier'. I rashly pointed out that not only were we tired but our food was not so good as that of Nippon soldiers. How I got away with this I do not know, but I had to eat my words and only got an extra couple of clouts for my impertinence!

On days like this we would leave the camp before light and rarely get back to it before dark. It meant that we could not get down to the river for a wash and were lucky if we could scrounge a pailful of water which a dozen of us would share for our ablutions. Often we would have to sit up until after 10 pm, waiting for the bucket of water to boil in order to have water in our bottles on the morrow, and that would mean a short night's sleep as we were always at work at five in the morning. No day would pass without some rain falling, so our clothes would always be wet through, and besides all this our tent leaked like a sieve.

By this time most of us were in pretty bad shape. There was scarcely a single man who was not suffering from either malaria, diarrhoea or tropical ulcers, but we had to go on working all the same. Each day tengko — the roll call at first light — would be a time of misery and anxiety for all concerned. The fit men would be silent, drawn up on the empty patch near the guard room, but the Korean warrant officer would be far from silent. 'Eighty men! Currah, currah! No eighty men? Why no eighty men? All men sick! Bugairo!' Seventy of the fitter would already be lined up while our M.O. made the decision whom to call out from among the waiting sick huddled together by the guard room, to make up the number required for the day shift.

On this particular day I don't know why, but I was one of the last of the day shift to leave the job. The night shift, poor devils, had already arrived and it was getting towards dusk. At any rate as I took the jungle path home I found myself on my own, a somewhat bizarre moment for a British POW in farthest Thailand.

Why ever it should have been I shall never know, but as I followed that track my spirits lightened. I looked about me with quickened interest in the last remaining minutes of daylight — and found myself actually singing! Don't laugh: it was a song from Mendelssohn's *Elijah* which I had learned at school. Could it be a sign of God's presence in the midst of all that suffering and misery? After all, no one else could hear me singing.

> O rest in the Lord,
> Wait patiently for him:
> And he will give thee
> Thy heart's desire ...

During that terrible month of July, cholera had raged in Hintock Jungle camp. Death came within 24 or 36 hours and bodies had to be burned on huge pyres. Teddie Wolfe was among those who succumbed and I was desolated by his death on the 26th when I learned of it through a ration party a few days later. Inevitably this

115

awful disease spread to our camp at Hintock River and by the end of that same month we had lost 40 men out of our group of 200. Then on the 3rd August a big party of sick arrived from the upper camp. I took my chance, volunteered to help in the hospital area, and the very next day was detailed to begin, together with four friends, Malayans from the FMSVF whom I had got to know in Changi: Pete Burne, Mat Urquhart, Andy Miller, and a few days later Bobbie Brown. I did one day's gravedigging, quite eaten alive by sandflies and then mercifully was given nursing duties.

During the whole of August I worked in this capacity in charge of a group of 21 sick men who had been evacuated from the upper camp. Of course it was a godsend for me as it gave me a let-out from the killing work on the cutting, but having said that it was heartbreaking to see those boys dying one by one. They were mostly in their twenties, conscripts from the mining villages of the Rhondda, who had been pitched into battle with little training and no acclimatisation before the fall of Singapore. Not only were they very sick, sick with every sort of tropical and jungle sickness, but at the back of it of course was the grinding starvation accentuated by the terrible nature of the work on the railway. Perhaps the worst thing was the fact that practically every man was thoroughly demoralised, to the point where they had given up the will to live.

Three incidents from my days with Tent 13 are engraved forever on my memory. Captain Headley was padre to this group of Welsh 77th Heavy Ack-Ack, a Welshman himself and Welsh-speaking too. I knew him for a good man, though no doubt like the rest of us out of his depth in the degrading conditions of this camp. One of my patients was clearly dying: he had been raving and calling out that he wanted to die, and he was upsetting the others. This was where I thought the padre might help, and he came soon enough, bringing his Welsh prayer book. I stood by while the padre talked with the man and read the office called the Visitation of the Sick and prayed with him in Welsh. In time the sick man quietened down, but he was dead the next morning, and I wrapped him up the same way as the others.

One of my most pitiful cases was a young bombardier whose

name became symbolic to me: Freeman. He lay on the bamboo slats, to all intents and purposes naked, but covered with a square of dirty blanket. He had had dysentery but wasn't purging any more and was quite helpless. When I came to see him that morning to clean him up I turned him over and was appalled to see what I shall hope never to see again: maggots crawling in and out of his anus. I said nothing and did what I could but mentioned this to the M.O. as soon as I had the chance. 'Oh, you needn't worry about that,' he said. 'They are quite healthy things, and do a good job while they are about it!'

By next morning I need not have worried for Freeman, for he had died, leaving this world, maggots and all. But I felt sorry as I wrapped him up in his blanket and went to report his death to the M.O., as he seemed to be a spirit whom the degrading circumstances of that camp could not quench. He had been unable to speak, but had smiled his thanks to me to the end.

The last incident is related though very different. It happened to be a fine morning after rain, with the damp hillside steaming in the sunshine. Whether it was a Sunday or not I cannot say, but Padre Headley proposed to hold a Communion service on a patch of open ground between the hospital area and the other tented lines. Perhaps there were a dozen or so: it was a day like any other and the fit men would have been on shift at the cutting, so the men attending were those confined to camp by the M.O. or like myself helping as cooks or orderlies. The picture is as clear as if it took place yesterday: the padre with his chaplain's scarf, the ragged and emaciated men kneeling, if they could, to receive this sacrament of God's love. It was, after all, a sacrament of life and of peace.

I had taken Freeman's few personal possessions to the CQMS in the usual way, Army Pay Book, wallet, etc, but I kept, with permission, the heavy nickel Gillette razor, Army Issue, which I use to this day. I wouldn't want to part with it.

The rest of the Thailand episode can be briefly told. Eleven of my original 21 patients died, either at Hintock or, later on, at

Kanburi. By December there was only one survivor. About the 15th August a party of the remaining 'fit' from H force, concentrated at Hintock, left for a spell on the final section of the railway some 50 miles up the line. On the 27th the first party to be evacuated from Hintock River left for Kanburi and I felt quite desolate; there were now few really sick men to be looked after. The camp was breaking up and high time too.

And now a little miracle. During the past month I had been suffering from more or less continuous diarrhoea, when Captain Reiss, our M.O., gave me five M & B 693 tablets, to see if that would effect a cure. At that time this was considered to be a wonder drug and I was amazed that the doctor had any supplies left. The very same day the camp was suddenly notified of further evacuation and Captain Reiss agreed that I should be included. What immense relief to be leaving such a spot and such associations. The party left by barge in the afternoon, arriving at Tarso by dusk, and my diarrhoea was cured in a few hours! My diary records as follows:

13th Sept. Came down to Kanburi by train, leaving at 10 and arriving at 6.30 pm. The journey in open trucks, with Aussies, including Harry Russell, and buying all sorts of fruit, eggs, cakes and sweetmeats, was great fun. Met up with Pete Burne and the rest.

15th. Began work as nursing orderly in the H Force hospital camp, to which we are all evacuated. Conditions are semi-permanent huts with reasonable grub. Water is short, but there are plenty of opportunities for buying stuff if you have the money. Found Jack McEvett a skeleton with malaria and dysentery [he died a few days later]. John Peel, Len Morrison and Biddulph are now here.

22nd. Went down with fever, the first of three attacks. Bloodslide showed B.T. malaria.

Ten days before Christmas we were back in Singapore but, to our surprise, taken to Sime Road camp, very different from Changi. A new phase in our captivity had begun.

118

CHAPTER 18

THE TURNING POINT

The point of this book is not merely that it should be an account of my wartime experiences under the Japanese, nor the thrilling story of eventual reunion with Louise, but rather the unfolding of a life which had come under the influence of God. This new direction raised many searching questions: was it to lead me away from my chosen career abroad to a vocation for ministry in the Church? And how would that match up with Louise's expectations, should we ever be brought together again? How that came about will be discovered in the remaining chapters of this book, but it must not surprise you if you find the tone of what follows very different from what has gone before. I had, in a marked way, become a different person. My life had been turned upside down by the circumstances of war, while my thoughts were beginning to turn towards a goal which could not immediately find an affirmative response from Louise.

For me there was a turning point so definite that I have no difficulty in ascribing it to the heartrending and humbling circumstances which I faced at Hintock River and, in part, my brief but searing experience with those dying men placed in my charge in Tent 13. It was these experiences which led me to question the purpose of my life seen through my inability to cope adequately with the needs of sick and dying soldiers, and to wonder if the God who had preserved me so far had something more for me.

There is, too, an important difference in the writing of this narrative. While chapters 5 to 17 had been written up from diary notes by the close of 1945, the remainder represents my reflections over the fifty intervening years. And there has to be a lot more rain before the rainbow can be descried.

CHAPTER 19

NEW HORIZONS

Sime Road Camp, towards the centre of Singapore Island, a few miles out of the city itself, had been constructed as an R.A.F. hutted encampment before the outbreak of war. In better days it had been the principal golf course, and the old fairways had been preserved. It also had a pleasant climate, being near to the central forest reserve and the considerable inland lake formed by the McRitchie reservoir. Of special interest to me was the old golf clubhouse called the Green House, where Louise had briefly worked on her initial assignment to G.H.Q. Singapore back in December 1941. Now it had a different use as Japanese administrative H.Q.

By contrast with what we had endured in Thailand, Sime Road was heaven. The administration was light and the atmosphere relaxed. No vicious outside working parties were called for, but of course camp fatigues, gardening and wood-collecting parties were organised daily. For my part I was extremely lucky, and at the outset was detailed as assistant storeman to CQMS Tommy Atkinson whom I had come to know at Hintock River. He was a Lancashire man from Nelson, a mill-hand in civvy street, but a keen St. John Ambulance member, and so had risen to be Quartermaster in the R.A.M.C. He had a keen wit with plenty of salt, and initiative to a high degree. You might describe him as a great survivor. In time he also became a life-long friend.

Tommy, as 'Q' to Area 6 at Sime Road, quickly established a little empire, with myself as number two. We had a small hut for a store, with clothing our main responsibility, but control of certain items filtered from the few Red Cross parcels which came through from South Africa about this time, such as chocolate and cigarettes. We also had control of two 'camp cots', items affording great luxury after months of hard lying in gaol and jungle.

Around this hut I soon planted a vegetable garden and had the satisfaction of harvesting spinach and other small items to add to our diet. Tomato seeds carefully garnered from tins thrown out by some Italians (late prisoners brought in from a submarine which had taken refuge in Singapore) fruited successfully, but alas! I lost any ripening tomatoes to others who got in first. The important thing about the four months spent here was that, although rations were short, it provided a badly-needed break for men to recover a degree of fitness. For my part I found myself blessed by getting to know a number of new people in addition to Tommy Atkinson, whose friendship and wisdom altered my whole outlook and filled me with a new vision for the future.

The first of these was Kenneth Luke, a Malayan Volunteer like myself but in the FMSVF, a teacher in the Colonial Education Service: he too was facing a long separation from his wife whom he had married as the Japanese were rolling down the peninsula, so we found we had much in common. His warm and generous manner, his sense of fun, his balanced judgement and interest in spiritual matters, soon drew me to him, and we became friends for life. It was he who introduced me, early on in Sime Road, to a young Dutch officer, an engineer in the Dutch regular army who, with a number of colleagues from Java, had also been up-country in H Force. This new friend was Oswald Godin, a mystic and contemplative who loved his Bible and was remarkable in possessing certain spiritual gifts to a high degree. He never described himself as a medium and I never knew him to hold a spiritualist seance, but in the long evenings it was a delight to join in a circle with others and listen to him expounding a verse or text for example from the Book of Proverbs. No wonder I was intrigued and became extremely interested in his brand of spiritualism, although at the same time I was very wary because of my C. of E. upbringing.

To balance any excess of enthusiasm which Oswald might kindle within me, I became close to a Chaplain to the Forces, Padre Eric Cordingly (later suffragan Bishop of Thetford) who, with a light but charismatic touch, drew around him a number of men like myself. Some months later, when we had moved from Sime Road into Changi camp, Padre Duckworth, whom I had got to know so well in Pudu

121

Gaol, in a long conversation one evening, asked me casually if I had ever thought of becoming ordained. This really challenged me at a time when my character had been undergoing a tremendous change, and I had been reading a number of theological books, as the following extract from my diary reveals.

19th Sept. 1944. As a result of several talks with Duckworth, during which he suggested ordination as a possible goal for me, I attended a meeting of some dozen fellows who wish to have some instruction in the usual subjects that an ordinand is supposed to handle. Cordingly, Duckworth and Jones are running the course which is designed to be a practical one covering Prayer Book, Liturgy, Worship, Church History, Greek as well as Old and New Testament. I must say that although ordination has sometimes occurred to me as a possibility, and has existed, particularly during the last six months, as a germ at the back of my mind, it is still not more than that.

One further extract serves to illustrate the conflict in my mind at this time.

29th Sept. 1944. Had a splendid talk with Cordingly. Besides noting the details of my career, qualifications etc he got to the roots of my beliefs, my association with Oswald etc. He further pressed upon me my qualifications for the Ministry, and said he felt sure that I would become filled with the conviction that ordination was the only possible way for me ... since then I have felt strangely unsettled, day and night. My thoughts *will* continue to hover round this question. My career in the Colonies, in Malaya, seems to have been thrust willy-nilly into the background, and whether I want it or not, I feel I am being drawn towards this new idea.

By the beginning of October 1944 I became certain in my mind that I would be ready to offer myself for ordination at the end of the war if the call to this vocation remained clear and compelling. In reaching this position there were two factors, first the insistent voice of conscience prodding me on, and secondly the fear of a cool response or possible outright rejection from Louise when we eventually came together. While my determination to leave the Colonial Service and go for ordination was dominant, I knew I had to hold everything in tension and discover what had been happening to her in her separate life in the meantime.

CHAPTER 20

LINES OF COMMUNICATION

To the difficulties of separation from one's wife, common of course in this mixed up world of ours, whether in conditions of peace or war, were added the problems of communication, or rather lack of communication. The Japanese Government was not a signatory to the Geneva Convention which aimed to establish certain humanitarian principles governing the rights of individuals in time of war, with the result that the International Red Cross could not exert the same influence in the Far East as it did in Europe. The sending and receiving of letters remained extremely difficult for us in South East Asia throughout the war, since the postal arrangements for POWs and their dependents across the globe were precarious and patchy. We gathered that letters were routed through neutral countries like Portugal and by means of neutral shipping, but many fellow POWs received nothing for the duration of the hostilities and naturally this did not help morale.

In this exasperating situation I counted myself extremely fortunate compared with others, since I received no fewer than a dozen full-page letters and some shorter 25-word messages from Louise spread over the years 1943-5, and about the same number from my mother and other close friends. On her side Louise did not fare so well. For nearly two years there was nothing, then on Christmas Eve of 1943 my postcard written from Changi Barracks in February of that year reached her family in England, when the good news was immediately cabled to Australia. This historical communication with the enigmatic signature which caused so much interest is reproduced on page 146. In all the remaining months Louise received only one further postcard before the Japanese surrender, after which a degree of communication was resumed.

But there was one occasion of particular interest to my family which I mention here. It so happened that in August 1942 an English civilian named Valentine Peters, who had been working in Thailand as a mining engineer, was lodged briefly in Pudu Gaol before being taken, with other civilians, to the internment camp then at Changi Gaol, Singapore, and I had the good luck to meet him. I had not known him before, but we quickly established a family connection when we discovered that we were second cousins on my mother's side. After his arrival in Changi Gaol he was able to insert my name among a list of survivors which was later broadcast from Australia, and this was duly picked up by my family in England in August 1943. I must add that this led to some confusion as to my status, as it was assumed from the origin of the radio message that I was among civilian internees and not a POW.

Although I was greatly heartened by the letters and messages I received from Louise, however haphazard their arrival, the burning questions remained: where was she? what was she doing? what was her life-style? and so on. Her letters (which I began to receive in March 1943) showed that she had safely reached Australia and was employed by the same or similar set-up as that in Java. She gave the address of her uncle Walter Homewood in Sydney as a poste restante, and that was a great relief to me, as I could at least focus my thoughts on the Southern rather than the Northern hemisphere during the subsequent months. Treasured beyond all else was a photograph of Louise which reached me in Changi Gaol in December 1944. She wore a smart tailored suit with a star in her lapel which gave rise to endless speculation. I thought it quite stunning.

CHAPTER 21

A NEW PROSPECT

I now come to what is the most difficult chapter for me to write, since in a few pages I have to describe a change in my outlook which, to put it squarely, is dominated by the Cross. It was not a sudden conversion, for I was already a committed Christian as I understood things then. Rather it was a change in intensity pointing me away from the course of service to which I had been appointed, to a different kind of service in the name of Christ.

This change is clearly mapped out in my diary between January 1944 and August 1945 which suddenly becomes full and detailed, with many entries explaining developments particularly meant for Louise's eyes in due course. To read these now might show what an intolerably priggish person I would appear to have become, but this would not be true because I never saw my faith as cutting me off from life in any way at all or making me different from other folk.

What is really remarkable about this space in my POW career is the number of gifted, intelligent and devoted men who, in the astonishing freedom of that spell at Sime Road and later, played their part in developing my interest in all aspects of Christian faith and life: Oswald Godin, with his low profile and understated spiritualism; Eric Cordingly with his essentially Catholic approach and liberal High Church background; Ron Wait, a Methodist minister with a burning and sometimes tortured faith; these all influenced me profoundly in their several ways and together contributed to the shaping of my future. It was however Noël Duckworth who actually pointed me towards ordination.

So I read widely from the amazing collective library of the camp: Church History, Liturgy, books on prayer, biographies of saints, etc. I took to attending Holy Communion every morning in our camp 'church' when I could, not at all a bad thing when surviving on starvation rations, held my first service one evening under

Cordingly's guidance, and in the course of many wonderful evenings sat at the feet of one or other of these mentors I have named, and began to have a vision of what God might be calling me to do when the day of freedom dawned.

Freedom! This was the abiding thought, the tremendous hope which filled every man's mind during these days, built up little by little through what we might dredge from the local press, the *Shonan Times*, that dreadful vehicle of Japanese lies and propaganda, encouraged by every tiny whisper which our camp command would allow to emerge from the BBC broadcasts received through secret radios, and the continual if sporadic reassurance of the way things were going, through restrained references in the letters we got.

In May 1944 we POWs were moved from Sime Road Camp to Changi Gaol enlarged by certain accretions outside, e.g. officers' lines, swelling that camp to extraordinary proportions. By a stroke of luck I got a job in the central cookhouse, the Gaol kitchen, and together with Kenneth Luke took charge of the cleansing department. Somehow, very subtly and imperceptibly, our quality of living improved. In any cookhouse, I believe it to be true, no matter how rigorous the rationing may be – and it certainly was in Changi – you could not help but fare that tiny bit better than your fellows outside. The growing of vegetables in the Gaol gardens was pressed forward intensively, the canteen system whereby outside purchasing was negotiated, the skill, perseverance and imagination of each POW to stretch and enhance his rations to the uttermost (by hook or crook) all contributed to our survival, though many suffered more and more from debilitating deficiency diseases. Red Cross parcels were unloaded by tons at the docks, only to be stored in go-downs, and most supplies of this kind remained in store until the end, apart from two or three derisory issues which, though stimulating at the time, only led to a sense of frustration in the long run.

For about twelve months I remained in the cookhouse, enjoying singular freedom outside working hours and continuing my 'education' much as before. Work parties continued with increasing pressure, the principal one being the construction of a totally new aerodrome at Changi Point. This was a huge undertaking for those days, even though the Japanese engineers used mechanised diggers, graders, etc, and it was killing for POWs to be employed upon it. It was never shift work as far as I recall, but to be 'on the drome' for eight or nine hours a day, under the burning sun or through heavy monsoon rain, was a type of slave-labour I was thankful to be spared. In fact I only ever did one day on the drome, and to this day I do not know why my name was never included in the detail for regular work upon it.

Months passed or rather dragged by, enlivened by a series of the most sparkling plays, revues and concerts which a most imaginative and gifted team of entertainers devised. For a change I went on the 'Coconut Party' now and again under Stan Weston of Malayan Fertilisers, one of my Volunteer friends from Kanburi days, but for me, after I left the cookhouse, it was mainly 'wood party', fetching in loads of rubber trees where twenty men would pull trailers up to four or five miles, bringing in the fuel to feed the insatiable furnaces powering the cookhouse boilers.

By June of 1945 a different atmosphere seemed to pervade the camp. We were filled with a kind of nervous expectation, as clearly were our captors, for suddenly new outside working parties were called for, 600 fit men comprising groups of 100 or so under the letters X and Y. My diary records that, at the end of May, 105 men were pulled out of the cookhouse (and elsewhere no doubt), myself included, specifically to make up the numbers for these parties. We were placed on standby in separate billets, but strangely enough orders to move were not given for several weeks. Throughout the month of June, therefore, we existed in a state of uncertainty, not knowing where we were heading or what the work would be.

This eventually proved to be part of a 'last ditch' defence scheme which the Japs were pushing ahead with in the expectation of an allied invasion of the Malay Peninsula and Singapore and, as we were shortly to find out, we POWs were to be employed on digging fox-holes for the I.J.A. in various locations on the North of the Island as well as in South Johore (on the mainland). It was not until the 28th July that our group was taken at an hour's notice in two buses across the Island, to find ourselves quartered in four shop-houses just past

128

the Ford Works — the former car assembly factory — some seven or eight miles along the Bukit Timah road. There we were joined by a small group of POWs from another camp, bringing the total of our work-party to 128 men and one officer.

By day these men, poor devils, were taken by truck to a rubber-plantation in South Johore, returning at dusk covered with red laterite mud, often with shocking tales of injuries received and death narrowly averted through insufficient pit-props to shore up the roof of the tunnels, resulting in numerous and dangerous roof-falls. Mercifully I escaped this hideous work as I was detailed to take charge of rations, messing and cooking. All this was a great responsibility as well as an anxiety, as I only got four hours' sleep a night, but two things came out of it. Firstly it brought me face to face with Japanese in a different way from hitherto, and secondly it provided opportunities to meet with POWs from other camps, as we met at St. Andrew's School to draw rations from the central store.

In general things could have been a lot worse and at any rate the feeding was on a much more generous scale than at Changi. However I have to say that I felt very isolated in this small work-party, without any fellow Volunteers, my only friend being a sterling Berkshire man named Jack Collins, from Chievely near Newbury, whom I had met earlier in the Cookhouse at Changi. His particular skill was as a hairdresser and barber and he shaved me regularly. One lasting thing I owe Jack Collins was that he persuaded me to change my parting from the left to the right-hand side, yet another change to face Louise with.

CHAPTER 22

THE SWORD OF DAMOCLES

What momentous days! What an astounding finish! The duration of Y Party, together with other similar groups, was cut short, providentially for us and all POWs in South East Asia, by the explosion of the Atom Bomb over Hiroshima, Japan, on Monday 6th August 1945. I say providentially, for subsequently evidence of the Japanese intention to carry out mass-killings of POWs was discovered and, horrid though the Atom Bomb was at the time and in its dreadful aftermath, there is little doubt that its use saved the lives of tens of thousands of allied POWs. Within a week Y Party had returned to base and we were thankfully reunited with our various parent units in the Gaol again.

My diary entry for the 29th August provides some interesting detail.

I am writing this back in Changi Gaol to which Y party returned on Monday 22nd August to find that almost all the Singapore working parties had already come in, as the result of hostilities having ceased between the Japanese Empire and the United Nations.

As a consequence of our isolation at Bukit Timah, we were ignorant of the developments which led up to the 'peace', and did not undergo the nerve-wracking time which the POWs in the Gaol experienced. Our first indication that the end was near was on the 16th August when I contacted some of the Pasir Panjang party when at St. Andrew's school. They told us of Russia's entry into the Japanese war and the Jap protest against the Atom Bomb. A day or two before, some of our boys on the tunnelling job were told by the Chinese about the Atom Bomb. The next thing was on the 17th when Jap Kempi officers stopped work on the tunnelling and one came into the camp and gave some instructions to the Nips in the workshops. These immediately set about sorting and burning their papers. By the atmosphere, the behaviour of the Nips, the state of the Bukit

Timah road, and by reports that 'All was over' from the Chinese outside, we all judged that something great and momentous had occurred. But what? Some thought it was invasion, others capitulation.

Work stopped for us on Friday. On Saturday we were told to stand by for return to Changi, and on Monday the 22nd, after two anxious and uncertain days, this took place in the afternoon, when we were taken by a roundabout way across the Island back to the Gaol, where we learned what had actually taken place. When we reached it the noise, the uproar in the Gaol was stupendous!

We were free! We had been liberated! But we were in the doldrums. Camp life continued as before, rations had to be drawn, meals prepared, fatigues of all sorts continued to be undertaken and outside parties for wood and gardening continued. Some ten days after hostilities ceased a small party was dropped in by parachute, a doctor and a few specialists to evaluate priorities. On the 5th September I saw the first evidence of a British presence, a cruiser lying off Keppel Harbour. Things were really beginning to happen!

While we waited for repatriation procedures to get under way, boredom was our chief enemy, so with my Thailand experience behind me I again volunteered as an orderly in the hospital, and to my delight was taken on as a dresser for Major Fagan, an Australian and a fine surgeon, who had done much brilliant work in camp hospitals on the Railway. I was happy and quite enjoyed swabbing out enormous or creeping ulcers and applying EUSOL dressings.

It was on such a morning, the 11th September, when I was busy on the ward, that I heard my name over the tannoy system. Would L/Cpl Mowat report to the Guard Room. Wondering what on earth this might be, dressed in an old pair of khaki shorts, I went along to be greeted by none other than an American officer who introduced himself as Maj. General H.H. Fuller, Deputy Chief of Staff to Lord Louis Mountbatten, the head of SEAC – South East Asia Command. Was I L/Cpl 80588 Mowat of the Straits Settlements Volunteer Force? I assented. 'Wa-al,' he drawled, 'I have some news for you. I saw your wife in Manila a month back. She is a Captain in the WAC

(Women's Army Corps) and she is serving as confidential secretary to General MacArthur's Deputy Chief of Staff out there. I offered to contact you if it were possible.'

My whole being surged with emotion at this amazing news and I didn't know what to say. The general then questioned me regarding my repatriation. To this I replied that I believed my wife to be in Australia and had asked for repatriation there accordingly. He said he would cable right away to Manila, with information of my safety and intention to be evacuated to Australia. The interview terminated with my thanks, a handshake and a salute, and I made my way back to the lines with my spirits going over the moon! A copy of the cable sent by General Fuller is reproduced (see Appendix).

Three weeks passed. I took the chance to visit Sime Road camp and met many former friends, among them David Gray MCS. Kenneth Luke was confirmed by the Bishop of Singapore. A colleague in the MCS, Bill James, on leave in February '41, had found his way into the R.A.F. and now as Squadron Leader James had tracked me down in Changi and introduced himself as a relation-by-marriage. This he was able to do, I may say, since my brother John had married Peggy Frame, sister to Janet who was now married to Bill. It was a bit complicated, but I didn't let it worry me. Far more important was that he invited me to return with him to Singapore where he was trying to get things going again in the former Chinese Protectorate. I did so and spent a fascinating 24 hours with him, also seeing other friends in town.

In retrospect the wait did not seem too weary. Fellow POWs — Volunteers who were seriously ill — were very soon air-lifted to Rangoon and on to London, among them Padre Petter now suffering from acute T.B. The first fit men to leave were taken by the *Oranje* for the UK on the 17th September. Numbers gradually dwindled at Changi while the food situation improved dramatically. Girls with shining faces in the uniform of the F.A.N.Y.S. appeared to hasten the process of repatriation under the acronym of RAPWI. Suddenly and thankfully it was all over and it was our turn. On Sunday the 23rd

This portrait of Louise taken in Melbourne in 1942 was received by Geoffrey in Changi prison on 17th December 1944. The 'U.S.' emblem underneath the star indicated that she was working in a civilian capacity for an American general.

80588 L/Cpl GEOFFREY SCOTT MOWAT
British Prisoner of War
Changi Camp

FROM: Mrs. G. S. Mowat,
c/o W. B. Homewood,
12 Dorchester House,
149 Macquarie Street,
SYDNEY, N.S.W., AUSTRALIA.

14 February 1945

Beloved Geof,

Thinking of you specially on this Valentine's Day.   Remember
Woodstock Road.   Next time we will celebrate our ninth together.
All my love, dear heart, from

Lulu

(MRS. G. S. MOWAT)

80588 L/Cpl GEOFFREY SCOTT MOWAT
British Prisoner of War
Changi Camp

From Mrs. G. S. Mowat,
c/o W. B. Homewood,
12 Dorchester House,
149 Macquarie Street,
SYDNEY, N.S.W., AUSTRALIA.

28 February 1945

Beloved Geof:

Jim has second son Peter.   John Evans married October.
Dreamed you walked in office yesterday.   Sure it will come true
one day soon, darling.   Love

Lulu

(MRS. G. S. MOWAT)

Louise on active service in Tacloban, New Guinea, drawn by an American War Artist, Sidney Simon, for her birthday, 24th December 1944

St. Paul's Church, Changi, built by POWs inside the walls of Changi Gaol. The author worshipped here regularly during 1944 and up to the time of the Japanese surrender on 16th August 1945.

September, together with a number of Volunteers and David Gray, we boarded the *Highland Chieftain*. We had chores of course, were over-fed no doubt, but how could we be bored? Before me, day by day, was the shining yet awesome prospect, that fateful meeting with Louise, who had been my wonder and my lode-star for the past three and a half years.

CHAPTER 23

OCEANS APART

(Louise writing)

If Geof was anxious I was, frankly, scared. Much water had flowed under the bridge since Geof and I had parted in Singapore in January '42 and the tide of war which had carried him off into captivity bore me by a series of little miracles in a different direction altogether. As a married woman I had some status, yet without the encumbrance of a family, and with my secretarial training I was free to use my skills as best I might in pursuance of the war effort. It was therefore providential that, having begun in G.H.Q in Singapore, I was able to continue in Java, and for the duration of the war was fortunate enough to be involved at the very hub of events in so far as the prosecution of the war in South East Asia was involved.

My wartime career, such as it was, ending up as already related in the American WAC, was in part due to my great friend Beryl Stevenson, an Australian girl who had run a typing school with great success in Wagga-Wagga. In 1939 she took a trip to England and on her way back met — and married — a British Army officer who had been posted to Singapore. This broke up her plans, but resulted in her finding work in GHQ Singapore, and in this way she became my friend and companion in Java and thereafter. The lightning course of the Japanese war and the fall of Singapore soon terminated the shadowy era of the combined military command in Java under General Wavell (ABDACOM), where we had been working. Within six weeks of arriving in Java, Beryl and I were fellow-travellers in flight from the enemy across the island to Tjilatjap on the west coast, whence we were brought by 'Shell' flying boat to land at Broome in West Australia, typewriter, baggage and all.

Our boss in Java, American Air Force General Brett, was true to his word: Beryl and I flew on to Melbourne via Alice Springs and on arrival were taken on as confidential secretaries. The scene quickly changed with General MacArthur's escape from Bataan in the Philippines and his arrival in Australia in March 1942. He moved the H.Q. from Melbourne to Sydney and then after only six months to Brisbane. By that time I had become confidential secretary to General Marshall, Deputy Chief of Staff under MacArthur. It was a happy posting, working with high-powered and intelligent men, and of course it enabled me to follow the progress of the war in the closest possible manner, and always with the thought of being in the right area if Geof should return alive.

This part of our story is not going to be half the length of Geof's, since the purpose of this book is to follow God's mysterious ways of working his pattern out, and eventually to see 'the Rainbow through the Rain' in spite of the difficulties, humanly speaking, which were put in our way.

The plain fact of the matter was that I had a picture and an understanding of Geof in my mind for all the three and a half years we were separated, and in my mind was the sole and strong desire to get together, start a family and resume what I thought would be the 'old life' on return to Malaya after the war was over. When, therefore, while still in Manila, I received the very first letter from Geof written from Changi after the Japanese surrender, in which he intimated that he felt strongly drawn to a vocation in the ministry of the church, perhaps I might be forgiven for expressing a reserve very strongly in the negative. In the years we had been, as it were, oceans apart, not merely in our separation but in our circumstances and manner of life and thinking, we had developed in such different directions and among such a different body of friends, it was not altogether surprising that I put my point of view so vehemently to Geof when I met him in due course. Our married life together and family must come first, I said, but I could not go along with his call.

I had been in General Marshall's office for the best part of two and a half years, and during that time General MacArthur's strategy for leap-frogging the Japanese defensive position in the islands of the South West Pacific had been remarkably successful. The point came in mid-1944 when, as a civilian, I would no longer be able to continue in my role, since the next move would not be a step but rather a leap, from Brisbane, Queensland to Hollandia in Dutch New Guinea. This represented a sphere of active service outside the mainland of Australia, and only those women in nursing units were allowed to go. In discussion about this with General Marshall I was offered the possibility of going into uniform as a WAC and the question was duly put before the C. in C. himself. 'What is her marital status?' the General asked. General Marshall replied that it was believed that her husband was a POW of the Japanese. The matter was settled. I had approval from the top for my gazetting as Lieutenant in the WAC and within a matter of weeks flew to Hollandia, the capital of Dutch New Guinea, in the N.E.I., to be briefly there under canvas but, very soon, following American successes, to fly on to Tacloban in Leyte Island — the Philippines at last!

From there to Manila seemed but a short step, and to my last wartime billet in that war-torn city. With a group of some dozen other WAC officers we were lodged in a fine private house in the suburbs belonging to an aristocratic mestizo family, and it was there in mid-September 1945 that I finally got word of Geof. My General could not have been kinder in making all necessary arrangements for bringing my time in Manila — and so my war service — to an end. For me it was most traumatic to have to say goodbye to so many fine people, both men and women, after years of working so closely together towards the ending of a war which even now was drawing to a close.

Within three weeks I was given orders to proceed to Sydney prior to my separation from the Service. In the meantime I was advised that the *Highland Chieftain* would probably reach Sydney on the 15th or 16th October. It was all 'go' and I was very nervous. My plane to Brisbane was delayed 24 hours by a heavy tropical storm which caused us to divert to Rockhampton in Northern Queensland and when I went into my tailor's to have my medal bars and ribbons fixed I learned to my great dismay that Geof's ship had passed through the day before and would be docking in Sydney the very next day. What could I do? A flight to Sydney was impossible that afternoon, but I took the precaution of alerting the general in charge of the American base — who was a friend of mine — to Geof's likely arrival before I could get to the scene.

Here I have to say how wonderful my friends were in what they did, far beyond the limits of the Service, in bringing Geof and me finally together. Maj. General Donaldson sent his aide to the ship to tell Geof what had happened. Some hours later, towards evening, he sent a car to bring Geof to the airport in time to meet my plane as it taxied on to the runway. It was the 11th October 1945 and the billet reserved in Sydney's best hotel — a double billet — was full of red roses and carnations.

CHAPTER 24

BITING THE BULLET

(Geoffrey resumes)

The roses and carnations were magnificent and our room at Usher's was beyond my imagining after the deprivations of 'camp'. All Louise's many friends welcomed us both generously and unaffectedly, and this wonderful support together with the needs and disciplines of each succeeding day (my medicals were seen to by the British Navy) and the tireless search for shipping to bring us back to England helped to give some sort of framework to this strange new existence. It is true I had a really bad feeling at the pit of my stomach when Louise stepped off the plane. She was looking wonderful and so trim in her uniform, and had the ribbon of the Legion of Merit and the Philippine Medal to show for her years away. In her manner eagerness battled with shyness as we embraced and of course I was immensely proud of her.

I was amazed at the wide circle of her friends both in Sydney and in Melbourne and really enjoyed meeting them: this was Louise's home ground where she had all the advantage and I was starting from scratch. It was hard work for me both mentally and emotionally, for I was struggling to overcome the lostness and alienation of leaving my former protected if limited existence, and to build up a self confidence which, initially, was so poor that, for example, it required a tremendous effort of will even to lift the bedside telephone and ask for room service.

As I look back I can see how all that was good and necessary. It was a time to grow together again. Talk, talk, talk – we had to talk together and did so endlessly, at any rate during our first night together. So much of Louise's experience poured out to fill the void of our long separation. On my side, what I had experienced seemed either so remote as to be irrelevant or so traumatic as to be beyond articulating, and indeed there were so many things which I felt were better kept to myself.

There was however one subject on which I simply could not remain silent for long. It had been burning in my breast for nearly two years, and my first post-POW letter to Louise had carried the gist of it. What would she say when at last I felt strong enough to open up the question of my call to ordination?

This is where the rain came down. I had to swallow very hard and keep my composure when a few days later, to my immense disappointment, Louise made it clear that she couldn't see things in my light: she had not married me to be a parson's wife, and looked forward to returning to a life abroad and starting a family.

The decision, then, to put on one side any thoughts regarding possible ordination was entirely mine, and the whole question remained a secret between us for a long time. There was, however, one person in whom I felt I had to confide, and so perhaps find a release from any lingering doubts or feelings of guilt. This was Eric Cordingly, and in due course Louise and I arranged to meet him some months later on our return to England. He was by then restored to health and back again with his wife and family at the Rectory, Leckhampton.

Cordingly, I may say, not only showed his full understanding of what had passed between Louise and me back in the early days of our reunion in Sydney, but he was also quite forthright in his comment. 'Geoffrey', he said, 'there's no doubt in the least that you had a call — and a genuine call to ministry. I know full well that you responded to it in all sincerity. If God now wishes you to return to colonial life and build up your family, that's wonderful. But remember, the One who has called you may not easily let you go!'

Eventually I became reconciled to resuming my career in the Malayan Civil Service, and returned to duty in Kuala Lumpur in May 1946, putting everything else behind me. But the call continued to remain at the back of my mind over the succeeding years and did not go away.

.   .   .   .   .   .

I think that every reader of this book will know what I mean when I say that it was like a red rag to a bull. I refer to the Japanese flag, a red sun on a white background. For a long, long time it was for me a symbol of all that was horrid and hated concerning the Japanese occupation and I could not bear to see it displayed without it causing a red rage of burning anger to well up within me. This unfortunate response to the sight of the flag of a free Japan persisted until I became District Officer at Butterworth in 1952, for in that position I frequently had to make the crossing from Butterworth to Georgetown (Penang) in the course of official duties, and I would find myself quite upset whenever I saw a ship flying the Japanese flag in the roadsteads.

Some three years later, when I had been posted to the State Secretariat at Negri Sembilan, as Senior Lands Officer, I was brought face to face with the whole issue by a telephone call from Singapore. The Malay clerk on the switchboard said there was a call from – the Japanese Consul in Singapore: would I take it? I drew a deep breath and said yes, and listened with a fast-beating heart hammering within me, while a voice at the other end explained that this was an enquiry about the marking of certain Japanese graves located on the hillside above the town.

I dealt with this routine matter in what I trusted was a cool official way, but inside I was in a turmoil. This sort of thing just could not go on, and from that day I prayed that God would change my attitude if I could not effect the change I sought myself. And I believe he did; for when the Independence of Malaya was looming, and the opening came a year later to offer myself for the ministry through the Bishop of Singapore, I don't think I would have been accepted unless I had taken the first step along the road to forgiveness, which is the base-line of the Christian faith.

Bath, 23rd April 1995

140

EPILOGUE

If this book has been long in the making, it has been because we've learned to live in God's time, not ours. We've learned of family, of stewardship, of saying yes to God's voice calling us, first to one thing, then to the next: always the leading, the compulsion, the gradual unfolding of what we cannot see but trust as part of what is beyond.

The decision to put a vocation to ministry behind Geoffrey in 1945 was not a lost decision, but a decision for a while: and in that time God was at work in other ways, shaping our family (two boys and two girls), building our loyalties to the country of our adoption and our bonds with fellow members of the Malayan Civil Service. These were fruitful years when service in district and secretariat alike was rewarding, fulfilling and satisfying.

In the course of our eighteen years in the Far East we formed many friendships, among all communities, which continue to this day, and we began to prepare for that inevitable severance which would bring us out of that beloved country for a while. The independence of Malaysia in 1957 was the end of an era for us, but it did bring Geoffrey the possibility of ministry as a second career, and when the Bishop of Singapore (Bishop Henry Wolfe Baines) agreed to support this, Louise was able to say yes.

Within a matter of weeks of leaving Malaya in January 1958 Geoffrey was back at College, but this time at Ripon Hall, Boar's Hill, Oxford, and was ordained Deacon at Bristol Cathedral at Trinity, 1959. These last thirty years and more, including a return to West Malaysia as a mission partner to that Diocese in 1977, have proved a wonderful time of ministry together, sharing God's grace in a world of conflict, turmoil — and glory!

Geoffrey and Louise
Bath, April 1995

MAP OF
BRITISH MALAYA
illustrating my captivity
under the Japanese
15 February 1942—15 August 1945

1942	15 Feb	Fall of Singapore.
	19 Feb	Escaped from Changi.
	29 Mar	Recaptured at Labis, Johore.
	Apr-Nov	In Kuala Lumpur gaol.
	Nov-Dec	Back to Changi by stages – Malacca, Muar, Johore.
1943	13 May	Sent to Thailand to work on Bangkok-Moulmein line.
	13 Dec	Returned to Singapore.
1944	9 May	12,000 P.O.W's concentrated in Changi gaol.
1945	16 Aug	VJ Day

China Sea

THAILAND

• Jitra
• Alor Star

KEDAH

• Kota Bahru

PENANG

KELANTAN

PERAK

Ipoh •

TRENGGANU

EAST COAST LINE
(taken up by Japanese)

• Kuala Lipis

Slim River •

• Gap

SELANGOR

PAHANG

• Bentong

KUALA LUMPUR •

NEGRI
SEMBILAN

Seremban •

Tampin •

GEMAS

SEGAMAT

Port Dickson •

MERSING

• A. Gajah

LABIS

MALACCA

MUAR

KLUANG

JOHORE

B. PAHAT

KOTA TINGGI

Straits of Malacca

JAHORE BAHRU

SUMATRA

SINGAPORE

KEY
```
...........  Singapore-Bankok
             Railway
— — —        State boundries
• • • • • •  Escape route
```

| 0 | 20 | 40 | 60 | 80 miles |

143

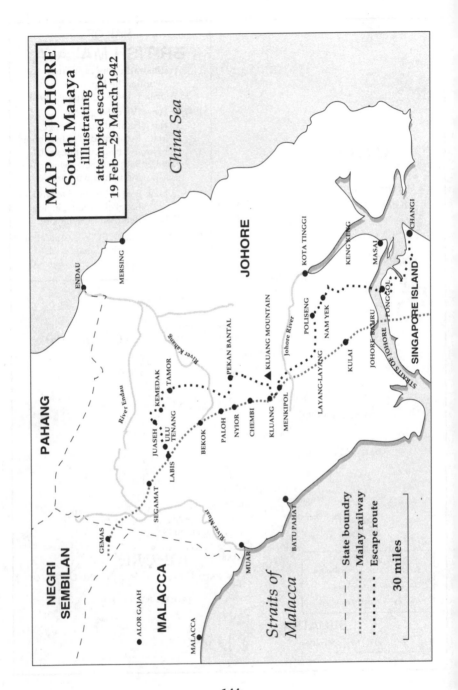

MAP OF JOHORE
South Malaya
illlustrating
attempted escape
19 Feb—29 March 1942

China Sea

JOHORE

PAHANG

NEGRI
SEMBILAN

MALACCA

Straits of
Malacca

Straits of Malacca

SINGAPORE ISLAND

CHANGI

KENG KENG

MASAI

PONGGOL

JOHORE BAHRU

KOTA TINGGI

POLISENG

NAM YEK

KULAI

LAYANG-LAYANG

MENKIPOL

KLUANG

KLUANG MOUNTAIN

Johore River

PEKAN BANTAL

TAMOR

KEMEDAK

JUASEH

ULU
TENANG

LABIS

CHEMBI

NYIOR

PALOH

BEKOK

SEGAMAT

GEMAS

MUAR

BATU PAHAT

ALOR GAJAH

MALACCA

River Muar

River Endau

River Kahang

ENDAU

MERSING

State boundry
Malay railway
Escape route

30 miles

144

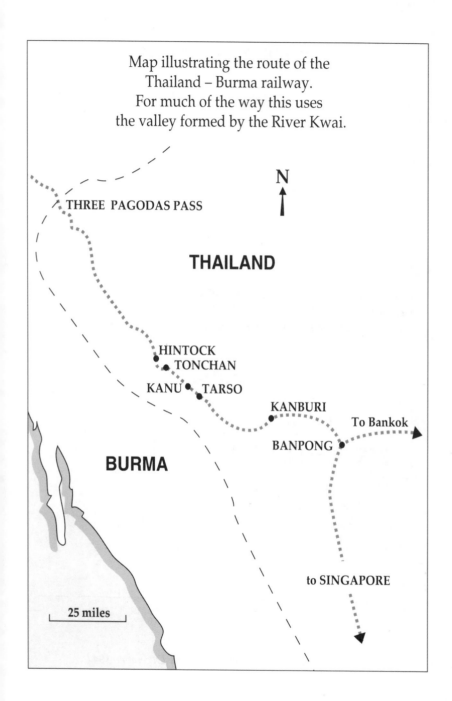

Map illustrating the route of the
Thailand – Burma railway.
For much of the way this uses
the valley formed by the River Kwai.

N

THREE PAGODAS PASS

THAILAND

HINTOCK
TONCHAN
KANU TARSO
KANBURI
BANPONG
To Bankok

BURMA

to SINGAPORE

25 miles

APPENDIX: DOCUMENTS

80588 L/CPL. G.S. MOWAT.

DARLING LULU,

I'M PRISONER OF WAR.

HEALTH, SPIRITS, EXCELLENT.

HAPPILY OCCUPIED AS PADRE

PETTER'S ORDERLY.

TIME FLIES FAST.

LOVING THOUGHTS FROM YOUR

OWN VAL.

The unusual signature on this twenty-five word postcard indicates that it was written on Valentine's Day, 1943. It was sent from Changi Camp and was received by Louise's parents in England in December 1943.

Ptg. 478/35.	POSTS AND TELEGRAPHS DEPARTMENT, MALAYA.	(P) & T.—Tg. 4)
LOCAL NO. {IN / OUT	**RECEIVING FORM.**	NO. OF TELEGRAM

CLASS

The first line of this Telegram contains the following particulars in the order named :
Number of Message, Office of Origin.
Number of Words, Date, Time handed in and Official instructions.

NO. O.O. ...... On Japan ...... NO. W. 30 DATE 22 TIME 11.40am

THIS FORM SHOULD ACCOMPANY ANY COMPLAINT OR ENQUIRY REGARDING THIS TELEGRAM.

TO Mowat District officer Grs
2ampm

Geof says come singapore wednesday by car to stay indefinitely room reserved raffles bring his thick socks visiting hours 4 to 6 birthday wishes Loch

RECEIVED AT 12/33 FROM HC BY KW   SENT AT ...... TO ...... BY ......

18185—970/200 p—8-10-40—R 36/13.

Telegram from Loch to Mowat, 22nd December 1941

146

GENERAL HEADQUARTERS, U. S. ARMY FORCES, PACIFIC
ADJUTANT GENERAL'S OFFICE
RADIO AND CABLE CENTER

INCOMING MESSAGE
IN THE CLEAR
ROUTINE

12 September 1945

TO   : PERSONAL FOR MAJOR GENERAL RICHARD MARSHALL

FROM : SACSEA REAR

NR   : 120613 Z

Jeoffrey Scott Mowat in splendid shape and best of spirits. Visited Prison and saw him personally. He will arrive in Sydney Australia about 16th October. Mine was first news he had had of Captain Mowat in over a year. Delighted over Captain's work. So happy impossible for him to talk.

FULLER

TOO: 120613 Z

MCN: ZUA 99

DISTRIBUTION:

DEPUTY CHIEF OF STAFF - INFORMATION

10649

ROUTINE
IN THE CLEAR

AFPAC AGO
Form No. 108
1334—AG Printing Plant—8-10-45—510M

1
COPY NO.

147

While serving in the Malayan Union Secretariat, Kuala Lumpur, I wrote the following testimonial, dated 21st August 1946, in response to a request from the Inspector of Prisons to substantiate my signature which appeared on a letter written in Tamil to Suppiah, sub-warder at Malacca Gaol, during the Japanese occupation.

MEMORANDUM

In November, 1942, I was one of a party of 100 British P.O.Ws. who were brought to Malacca Gaol by the Japanese. We were crowded into a small section of the Gaol for a fortnight, during which period we were looked after by the Prison Staff with every possible courtesy and kindness.

2. In particular Sub-warder Suppiah who was in charge of the Kitchen while we were there, spared no pains in seeing that we had the best food and cooking and attention that was at his disposal. I was very much impressed by Suppiah's devotion and loyalty to us although we were P.O.Ws., and it was in thanks for all he had done for us while we were in the Gaol that Mr. Morrison wrote the letter in Tamil at (1B), to which I subscribed my name.

3. I would like to end this memo. with a tribute to Mr. Marbeck who in his capacity as Prison Dresser, was virtual head of the Prison at the time, and through whose efforts it was that we were left alone by the Japanese while in custody there. I cannot speak too highly of what he and the others on the Prison Staff did for us at great risk to their own personal safety.

(signed) G. S. MOWAT
Assistant Secretary
Malayan Union Secretariat
21.8.1946

| Communications should be addressed to:— |
| THE UNDER-SECRETARY OF STATE. |

Your reference ....

C.O. reference ....10001/45............

COLONIAL OFFICE,

(ENQUIRIES AND CASUALTIES DEPT.),

2, PARK STREET,

W.1.

(Tel. : MAYfair 8166).

15 SEP 1945

Sir,
~~Madam,~~

I am directed by the Secretary of State for the Colonies
to inform you that he has just learned with great pleasure
that

2588   L/CPL. G. S. Howat   S.S.V.F.

has been released from internment in Changi Camp.
Singapore on 5ᵗ September 1945.

Camp.   His state of health ~~is said to be~~
          Her   has not yet been reported.

I am, Sir,

your obedient servant,

Rob. Hardleigh.

J. B. Homeward Esq.

Golden Wedding, 7th July 1990

INDEX AND GLOSSARY

along the contours on hilly rubber estates to check erosion 26

Simpson-Gray, L.C.: Malayan Civil Service (1926-1942). Barrister Middle Temple. Labour and legal posts. D.O., Tampin, Negri Sembilan, 1942. Missing, attempting to escape after the capitulation 17

Smith, F.M., CBE: Malayan Civil Service (1937-62). Prewar appointments include Kuala Pilah, Malaca, Selangor Secretariat. Commissioned Malay Regiment, 1941: wounded in action: POW Singapore, Thailand. Postwar appointments: B.A. Perlis, B.A. Trengganu, Perm. Sec. Ministry of Internal Security. In retirement took up teaching mathematics 11

Stevenson, Beryl: evacuated from Singapore to Java in company with Louise Mowat, in naval supply vessel *Anking*, 13 Jan. 1942. Conf. Secretary in ABDACOM (q.v.). One of some six British women commissioned in American WAC. Personal Secretary to Maj. Gen. Kenney, commanding U.S. Air Force in S.W. Pacific. Promoted Major. Legion of Merit and Philippine Medal 19

Subfusc: sober clothing, black or grey, required for the University examinations at Oxford 7

Surat: Malay for a written letter, often used as a reference from an employer 47

Susah: Malay meaning 'difficult', 'trouble'

Terang Bulan: Malay for full moon 64

Towkay: Chinese term for a wealthy person, land-owner, shopkeeper, employer of labour, etc

Tuan: Malay for 'sir', 'mister' 62

Turner, G.E.: Malayan Civil Service 1931-57: Tamil Dept. of Labour FMS and S.S. Pte Malacca Volunteeers. POW Burma/Siam Railway 11

Ulu: Malay, sometimes spelled 'hulu', meaning headwaters of a river, hinterland, 'upcountry' 47

Urquhart, Mat: tin mining engineer. FMSVF Armoured Car Squadron. POW Singapore, Changi Barracks and Changi Gaol; H Force, Thailand 116

Wait, the Rev. Ronald: a Methodist Minister pre-war, but serving as a commissioned officer in the army. POW Singapore, Changi Gaol 126

Walters, John: 1st Bn. S.S.V.F. Chartered Bank. Taught